ALSO BY STEVE SPRINGER

Winnin' Times: The Magical Journey of the Los Angeles Lakers
(with Scott Ostler)

60 Years of USC-UCLA Football (with Michael Arkush)

The Los Angeles Times Encyclopedia of the Lakers

Fred Claire: My 30 Years in Dodger Blue (with Fred Claire)

*Chick: His Unpublished Memoirs and
the Memories of Those Who Knew Him*
(with Chick Hearn)

American Son: My Story (with Oscar De La Hoya)

Laker Girl (with Jeanie Buss)

Historic Photos of USC Football

Hard Luck: The Triumph and Tragedy of "Irish" Jerry Quarry
(with Blake Chavez)

100 Things Lakers Fans Should Know & Do Before They Die

CAPTAIN PHIL
HARRIS

The Legendary Crab Fisherman,
Our Hero, Our Dad

JOSH HARRIS AND
JAKE HARRIS

with Steve Springer and Blake Chavez

SIMON & SCHUSTER

New York   London   Toronto   Sydney   New Delhi

Simon & Schuster
1230 Avenue of the Americas
New York, NY 10020

First Simon & Schuster hardcover edition April 2013

SIMON & SCHUSTER and colophon are registered trademarks of Simon & Schuster, Inc.

For information about special discounts for bulk purchases, please contact Simon & Schuster Special Sales at 1-866-506-1949 or business@simonandschuster.com.

The Simon & Schuster Speakers Bureau can bring authors to your live event. For more information or to book an event contact the Simon & Schuster Speakers Bureau at 1-866-248-3049 or visit our website at www.simonspeakers.com.

Designed by Ruth Lee-Mui

Manufactured in the United States of America

10 9 8 7 6 5 4 3 2

Library of Congress Cataloging-in-Publication Data

Harris, Josh.
    Captain Phil Harris : the legendary crab fisherman, our hero, our Dad / Josh and Jake Harris ; with Steve Springer and Blake Chavez.
        p. cm.
    1. Harris, Phil, 1956–2010. 2. Fishers—Bering Sea—Biography. 3. Ship captains—United States—Biography. 4. Crabbing—Alaska—Biography. 5. Cornelia Marie (Crab boat). 6. Fishers—Alaska—Biography. 7. Crab fisheries—Alaska. 8. Crab fisheries—Bering Sea. 9. Crabbing—Employment—Bering Sea. I. Harris, Jake. II. Springer, Steve. III. Chavez, Blake. IV. Title.
SH380.45.A4H47   2013
639'.56—dc23   2012042464

ISBN 978-1-4516-6604-5
ISBN 978-1-4516-6608-3 (ebook)

This book is for all the *Deadliest Catch* fans who supported the old man from day one. You all saw in our Dad the same thing we saw in him every day of our lives. You welcomed him into your living rooms each Tuesday night with open arms and made him a part of your family. Dad was always so appreciative and thankful to all the fans around the world. You were all there when we lost him, and we think of you as our extended family.
Dad's spirit will live on forever.

As Dad always said:

You can watch things happen . . .
You can make things happen . . .
Or you can wonder what the fuck happened . . .

We've taken Dad's words to heart, and we hope you all do the same in your lives.

We thank you for all your love and support.

Josh and Jake Harris

CONTENTS

FOREWORD

Everybody who watches *Deadliest Catch* knows Phil Harris. They watched him successfully navigate the *Cornelia Marie* through the Bering Sea in horrendous conditions, keeping his boat upright and functioning despite towering waves and mountains of ice. They saw him pull upward of a million tons of crab out of the water over the years, filling his quota in good times and bad. They admired his ability to mold a crew of tough, independent-minded deckhands into an efficient team, becoming the father figure for a floating family of fishermen.

Viewers laughed at his jokes, felt the force of his dominating personality, and were left in awe of his courage.

And then they cried when he died way too soon at fifty-three.

But Phil, our dad, wasn't a TV character created by a writer and portrayed by an actor. He was a real person with a family, a history, and a life off camera every bit as intense and entertaining as the one seen worldwide on Discovery Channel.

That was the Phil Harris that TV viewers never saw.

Three years after his death, we feel it's time his millions of fans get to know the man behind the legend. That's why we have written this book.

In these pages, readers will meet Grant, our grandfather, the first member of our family to shove off from land, setting us on a course through the Bering Sea that has been followed for three generations.

Our father didn't just materialize in a ship's wheelhouse. Here, readers will see his struggles, doubts, and fears as he overcame the many obstacles that separated him from his dream of becoming a crab boat captain.

At the age of eight, he lost his mother to cancer. In high school, he was voted Least Likely to Succeed. The men whom Dad fished with on his first boat also put him in that category. They only took him on board because he agreed to work for free. He was the greenhorn, the lowest position on the boat, and his first captain mocked him, predicting for all to hear that he wouldn't last.

That was enough to instill in Dad the determination to prove them all wrong. And his resolve still drove him long after he had succeeded beyond all expectations to become the most respected captain in the entire Bering Sea crab fleet.

When executive producer Thom Beers began *Deadliest Catch* in 2005, it was immediately clear to him that Dad was the logical choice to be the leading man in the series.

Readers of this book will learn about our father's life on land from his crazy days in Dutch Harbor, Alaska, to the back roads of his hometown, Bothell, Washington, where he was every bit as much a folk hero in the seat of his Harley or one of his Corvettes as he was on the top deck of the *Cornelia Marie*.

We will bring our mother, Mary, into the spotlight for the first time along with the many buddies who ran with Dad over the years.

We want to show how he was as a husband, a father, and a friend. We want people to know why he was our hero as well, and we'll share all that we learned from him that we will carry with us the rest of our lives.

And we want people to know that, while he may have led a wild life on shore, when the *Cornelia Marie* or any of the other boats Dad skippered left the safety of a harbor for the dangerous waters of the Bering, he was a serious, dedicated, accomplished captain, revered among his peers. The number-one responsibility of any captain is to bring his boat and crew back safely, and no one took that obligation more seriously than Dad.

He never let his desire for full pots of crab override his determination to steer his boat into the safest position to retrieve his catch. Though he obviously felt a special closeness for us, his sons, above all the other members of his crew, he was just as concerned with their well-being as he was with ours.

When it came to finding the crab, nobody was more skilled than Dad. Every captain has his methods and his secret locations, but our father's seemed the most rewarding.

Not a day goes by for either of us, no matter where we are in the world, without someone coming up and telling us how much he misses seeing our dad. We hope that, for all his fans, this book will in some small way bring him back to life.

To tell this story, we have enlisted the aid of *New York Times* best-selling author Steve Springer and fellow writer Blake Chavez. They have talked to the key people in Dad's life and are presenting a picture of him that, while not always flattering, is honest and inspiring. He wouldn't want it any other way.

Like Dad always said, "When it comes to my life, nothing is out of bounds."

So here it is, the Phil Harris you thought you knew, and the Phil Harris you will be seeing for the first time.

—Josh and Jake Harris

CAPTAIN PHIL
HARRIS

PROLOGUE

The mystic northern lights dance a scintillating, supernatural neon jig in the Alaskan sky.

God's country.

But stray farther to the southwest and the stark beauty of this little corner near the top of the world can lose its appeal to all but the hardiest of travelers. The terrain is rougher, the area barely habitable, the surrounding water even more menacing.

These are the Aleutian Islands, bordering on the Bering Sea, where the brave souls who challenge the harsh conditions share the area with polar bears, sea otters, and bald eagles, just a sliver of the population that includes twenty-five varieties of marine mammals, hundreds of invertebrate species, 110 million birds representing forty species, and 450 different kinds of fish.

Most of the people who venture into this frontier are part of the fishing industry. Some work in one of the area's many processing plants. Others man the fishing fleet that braves the notorious Bering Sea.

The fishing vessels are not of the ilk favored by commercial fishermen on the East Coast of the United States. Crab boats on the Bering Sea are more than 100 feet long, some stretching to more than 180. East Coast boats are normally one-quarter that length. The larger size is necessary to face waves that can soar as high as a four-story building.

Suffice it to say that a different breed of men fish the Bering Sea.

The crab fishing grounds encompass much of the 884,900 square miles of the Bering, the third-largest sea in the world. It is the northern-most region of the Pacific Ocean, bounded by Russia, Alaska, the Aleutian Islands, and the Bering Strait, beyond which is the Arctic Ocean.

The Bering has long been an enigma to those who ply her waters, a sea with a split personality. On any given day, the water may be as smooth as glass with a gentle breeze stirring the call of seagulls in the distance. On these occasions, the sea is nothing less than majestic. Sea otters float lazily on their backs, a whale swims in the distance, and seals, sea lions, and porpoises play as dolphins, a good omen to many sailors, race alongside an intruding fleet.

Within hours, though, the calm can be shattered, the beauty of a natural aquarium overshadowed by a deadly display of nature's power. A single arctic storm can range over a thousand square miles. The fishing fleets sometimes face hurricane-force winds, the strongest ever recorded in the Bering Sea reaching 159 miles per hour. Sets of waves, the highest ever seen estimated to be over 100 feet tall, can bring tens of thousands of gallons of water crashing onto the decks. Then there's the burglar of the sea that strikes when it is least expected: the rogue wave. It's a monster swirl that caves in against the grain of the sets rolling in, erupting in a wall of water.

And, as if the wind and water weren't trouble enough, there's the temperature. It can drop to forty below in winter, the prime season for crab fishing. When the mercury drops to such menacing levels, even the ocean spray freezes, and the deckhands are flayed with splinters of ice. Something as simple as urinating can be an adventure. When the crab boat crew does so outdoors under those frigid conditions, the urine freezes before it hits the deck.

There is ice everywhere on the boat: on the bow, the deck, the 800-pound crab-catching steel cages commonly known as pots, the ropes, the winch, even on the crew's moustaches. The layers of ice can weigh tons, which serves to make the boat top-heavy. As the ice builds up, the vessel becomes more and more likely to be rolled onto her side, a virtual death sentence for all aboard.

To avoid such a fate, the deckhands must break off the ice with sledgehammers. The crew can spend hours in the tough, urgent work of de-icing the boat. But often, once the ship is safe and fishing has commenced, the ice returns and the same chore must be performed again just hours later.

Boats on the Bering are mandated by law to keep a supply of outfits known as survival suits on board at all times. Crews are routinely tested by the Coast Guard to ensure they know how to put on this gear in a timely manner. Doing so in less than a minute is crucial to staying alive in the event that the craft sinks.

There is a general understanding between the Bering Sea and those who fish her: fall into her waters without a survival suit and you die.

There have been exceptions, but they are rare indeed. Anyone who tumbles into the water in subzero conditions can become paralyzed, as hypothermia sets in almost instantly. The vital body organs fail and the unfortunate soul finds himself in the throes of death within minutes.

That's usually not enough time for a rescue operation. Because of the great size of most crab boats, it takes the vessel almost ten minutes to maneuver a U-turn and come back. And if the seas are high or darkness has set in, the search for a lost crew member becomes even more difficult.

There are still more hazards to avoid. Rough seas and icy temperatures are the ideal conditions for the killer whales of the Bering Sea to go hunting. Nothing chills the soul like watching a whale just off the bow as it feasts on a great white shark.

4 | CAPTAIN PHIL HARRIS

Then, there are the icebergs. The *Titanic* didn't survive even a single confrontation with a mountainous mass of ice. Crabbers, in much smaller boats, face those huge killers every season. Sometimes the crabs congregate near the ice floes. And crabbers go where the crabs are.

Just being on board a crab boat is hazardous, but nobody is ever just on board. The fishermen are there to work, and their work is grueling. Take the brutal and seemingly never-ending task of stacking the eight-hundred-pound crab traps. Though a winch lifts the pots and delivers them on deck, they must be grounded so that the stacks are even and don't collapse onto the crew. Positioning the pots becomes a matter of muscle because they don't respond much to finesse. Even when they are properly stacked, the pots can tumble when they become caked with ice.

The bodies of crew members take a beating from head to toe. A crabber can expect to have his tailbone rubbed raw from slamming against the pots as he works. A bloody back and hindquarters are just part of the job.

The extreme changes in weather and temperature tend to wreak havoc on a deckhand's complexion. The toughened facial skin peels off in strips when exposed to extreme cold on such a regular basis.

The hands of a Bering Sea deckhand make those of a professional bull rider look manicured and pampered in comparison. Many deckhands are not able to retain all the digits on their hands. The fingers that survive grow gnarled, swollen, and misshapen. A crab boat deckhand sews his own stitches as readily as a carpenter applies a Band-Aid.

The dangers of such a job are reflected in data from the Bureau of Labor Statistics that ranks commercial fishing as the occupation with the highest fatality rate: 121.2 deaths per 100,000 workers, thirty-five times greater than the average for the overall American workforce. Loggers rank second with 102.4 fatalities per 100,000, followed by pilots and flight engineers at 57.0. The death rate for Bering Sea crabbers, in particular, is even higher still, at 260 per 100,000, according to a study by the National Institute for Occupational Safety and Health. Eighty percent of those Bering Sea fatalities are due to drowning or hypothermia.

Pound for pound, crabbers are the toughest bastards on earth.

This is the life that our father, Phillip Charles Harris, was destined for when he was brought into the world on December 19, 1956.

CHAPTER 1

SALTWATER IN HIS VEINS

It is dour; it freezes hard; it is difficult to navigate when the ice crowds down; and it punishes those who miscalculate its power. But it also teems with a rich animal life and rewards good hunters and fishermen enormously.

—*James Michener on the Bering Sea in his novel* Alaska

His name is on the lips of every man who has ever sailed north of the Aleutian Islands. But if Vitus Jonassen Bering's name had not been affixed to the Bering Sea, his role nearly three centuries ago in exploring the then-uncharted body of water would by now have been long forgotten.

Bering was a Danish-born sea captain who sailed under the Russian flag. It might seem strange that a foreigner would be given such a central role in the Russian navy, but it wasn't that unusual in an era when the Russian czar, Peter the Great, was always on the lookout for exceptional sailors. He wasn't concerned with their nationality, only their ability to help maintain his country's sea power.

Born in 1681 in Horsens, Jutland, the part of Denmark that connects it to the European continent, Bering took to the seas at the age of fifteen. In the next seven years, he sailed widely, reaching both the Danish East and West Indies.

He was looking for new horizons by age twenty-two, and he found them through Cornelius Cruys, a Norwegian who had become a vice admiral in the Russian navy and was, like Peter the Great, constantly in search of new nautical talent. Bering boarded his first Russian ship in 1703 and went on to distinguish himself in both the Great Northern War against Sweden and the Russo-Turkish War.

His military successes earned Bering the opportunity to take part in one of the great adventures of his age. Back then, much of the world, including Russia, didn't know if Asia and North America were separate continents or if they were connected by a land bridge. In 1725, Bering led an expedition to learn the answer while also searching for a northeast passage to China and exploring the possibilities for Russian trade and colonization in North America. He returned in 1730 to report that Asia and North America were indeed separated by a body of water, one that would later bear his name.

Three years later, Bering departed again on what became known as the Great Nordic Expedition, leading a group of as many as ten thousand on a journey that would last a decade, although he himself would not live to see the end of it.

In the summer of 1741, commanding his ship, the *St. Peter*, but separated by a storm from a sister ship, the *St. Paul*, Bering reached the coast of Alaska. On July 20, Georg Wilhelm Steller, a German naturalist, became the first European to set foot in Alaska when the *St. Peter* stopped at Kayak Island, east of Prince William Sound in the Gulf of Alaska.

He didn't get to stay long. Fearful of being stranded when winter arrived, Bering ordered Steller back to the ship and kept sailing, first north to the Alaska Peninsula, then west past the Aleutian Islands. But, despite his caution, Bering never made it back home. He was shipwrecked on an island just short of his destination, Russia's Kamchatka Peninsula. Suffering from starvation and scurvy, he died there along with twenty-eight crew members in December 1741.

But Bering will not soon be forgotten, because so much of the area—the Bering Sea, the Bering Strait, the Bering Land Bridge, and

Bering Island where he died—bears his name, a tribute to the man who reached Alaska decades before the United States even existed.

Over the centuries, many sea captains, Russian and American, have followed in his wake, venturing into the Bering Sea's treacherous waters and handing down the region's seafaring traditions from generation to generation.

For Grant Harris, though, there was no such family tradition, no notable lineage or treasured fishing lore. He didn't inherit a legacy, but he would certainly pass one on.

Grant, born in Seattle in 1933, never met his father. His parents were divorced and his father departed before he was born. Grant couldn't even claim his love of the sea was in his genes, since his father was a steelworker.

And even though he grew up in Seattle, a coastal city surrounded by water and home to a large fishing industry, Grant himself didn't leave dry land for a paycheck until he was twenty-seven. Before then, he had been an auto mechanic and worked in construction. He had always liked boats, but his interest was limited to canoes and rowboats.

Nonetheless, in 1961 Grant went to sea, going to work on the *Reefer II*, a boat that hauled frozen fish to processing plants up in Alaska. His five-year-old son, Phil, watched Grant leave on what must have seemed like a great adventure to the youngster.

"It was hard work," said Grant, "but when you're young, hard work doesn't mean too much. To me, the harder it was, the more challenging it became."

Perhaps the hardest thing of all, though, was his painful absence from his wife and young son. On that first trip, Grant was gone for six months.

There were many more such trips over the next four years. But over that period, the family adapted to the cycle and Grant learned to love the feel of the ocean and the essence of being a fisherman. He had found his life's work.

Only to lose the love of his life.

In 1964, his wife, Phyllis, just twenty-seven at the time, died of skin cancer. Her eight-year-old son, Phil, was devastated, left with a void that seemed impossible to fill. With his father out to sea for half of each year, Phil had forged a bond with his mother that he thought was unbreakable.

Both of his grandmothers tried to fill that black hole, serving as surrogate mothers, trying to make a trip to Grandma's house as special as they could. Whether it was showering Phil with gifts, making sure he did his homework, or nursing him through a cold, they were there, especially when Grant was working.

Grant, anxious to at least give his son the stability of familiar surroundings, didn't move from the family home in Bothell, Washington, even though, after Phyllis's death, every room in the house reminded him of her absence. Bothell was the only town Phil had ever known. A town of 2,200 back when Phil was growing up, Bothell, located twelve miles northeast of Seattle, has around 30,000 residents today. It's a quiet middle-class community where manufacturing and high-tech research and development are the leading industries.

Staying in Bothell gave Phil the benefit of attending the same school and keeping the same friends. But Grant knew that without Phyllis, he was going to have to do more. His own life was going to have to change: as a single parent, he couldn't spend months away in Alaska anymore.

"I wasn't just going to pawn Phil off on somebody else," Grant said.

But he wasn't willing to completely give up his life at sea, so he settled on a compromise. Rather than working for someone else, he would get a boat of his own, allowing him to fish when he pleased.

Along with a partner named Ralph Shumley, Grant leased a boat for the summer for salmon fishing in Bristol Bay, southwest of Anchorage. With the season starting in June, Grant took Phil out of school a little early so he could accompany his father up north.

The venture was so successful that, after two summers, Grant was ready to take the next step and buy a boat.

That seemed like a good idea until he went shopping. What he found on the market was too little in the way of quality and too much in the way of cost.

So Grant came up with a better idea: he would build his own boat. A marine architect designed the plans for the vessel, to be made of Alaskan yellow cedar.

During the daytime, Grant worked as a carpenter and handyman in the Seattle area. Every night and on weekends, he would go to nearby Lake Union to work on the boat, focusing his carpentry skills on the project that had become his passion.

On many days, he had a young helper. After school and on Saturdays and Sundays, Phil, ten by then, would go down to the lake with his dad as the ship took shape.

It was much-needed therapy for Phil, who was still getting over the loss of his mother. Ultimately, it was the lure of the sea that pulled Phil out of his grief and loneliness.

"While I was building the boat, I had Phil do a little bit of painting or a few other simple things he could handle as a youngster," Grant said. "The main thing was, I wanted him with me. At that age, you can't turn a kid loose. With his mother no longer around, I needed to know what he was up to."

Phil soon became a familiar sight around Lake Union. As he hopped from boat to boat, the stories of life at sea, the smell of the water, and the creaking of the ships all made a huge impression on his young mind.

It took Grant just seven months to complete his dream boat. He named it *The Provider* with the hope that it would be just that for his family.

Grant had the boat put on a freighter and shipped north to Bristol Bay, having adhered to that area's limit by making his boat thirty-two feet in length with a twelve-foot beam.

He got a job working for a fish processing plant and put the finishing touches on his craft at night. In June, when the fishing season opened, *The Provider* left Nushagak in search of king salmon, with co-owners Grant and Shumley on board along with the boat's junior crew member, Phil.

It was the beginning of a lifetime of fishing trips for Phil, though he could never have dreamed of that fate after that first outing—he absolutely hated it.

The summer fishing season coincided with baseball season. Phil loved the sport and wanted to be back home in Bothell playing with his friends.

Adding to his misery was the seasickness. The waves around Bristol Bay were nothing like the monsters Phil would later encounter in the midst of the Bering Sea. But at that age, it was more than he could handle. His solution was to try to sleep as much as possible on that trip, a luxury that would be unthinkable to Phil as an adult fisherman.

Grant, however, wouldn't allow his son to act like a passenger on a cruise, so he had Phil doing everything from handling the bait to helping unload the product of their labor.

"My grandpa didn't know how to raise a kid," Jake would later say, "so he raised a worker."

Grant didn't limit his fishing to salmon. He went up to Togiak, north of Bristol Bay, to catch herring, sold salmon eggs to a buyer in Hawaii, hauled fish, including silver salmon, to market, and captained charter boats.

In his many years at sea, Grant earned respect for his calmness in the face of danger, his determination to succeed no matter how daunting the task, and his carpentry skill.

Proof of that skill is *The Provider*. Grant sold it years ago, but it remains seaworthy to this day, moored in Seattle forty-five years after he built it by himself as a moonlighting project.

Grant doesn't brag about that, or anything else. He is a humble man who shuns the spotlight. Serene as a ripple-free pond, his emotions held in check, he is a man who speaks as if he has a limited supply of words. Yet he never fails to get his point across.

That's a stark contrast to his famous son, who relished his time in the eye of the camera. A type-A extrovert, Phil could be as explosive as the seas he sailed on, loud and nervous, sweeping through life as though driven by a swift current.

"They were such opposites," said Sig Hansen, captain of the *Northwestern*, "that when I met Grant and saw how quiet he was, I couldn't believe he was Phil's father."

Grant's judicious use of language was illustrated when he asked his grandson Jake, fifteen at the time, to pull down a fence in his pasture. Enjoying a bottle of soda out in the field before getting to work, Jake spotted an old coffee can and kicked it. To his surprise, a swarm of bees flew out and attacked him, stinging him five or six times.

In a panic, Jake decided on a drastic course of action to chase them away: setting the field on fire. The flames quickly spread, consuming about fifty square feet of grass.

Grant, working in a nearby shed, didn't know what had happened until he heard fire trucks, called by a neighbor, approaching with their sirens blaring.

"What in the hell are you doing?" Grant asked his grandson as the firemen extinguished the flames, avoiding further damage.

"Trying to chase those bees away," said Jake.

In typical Grant fashion, he succinctly replied, "I think you got them."

Grant's calmness served him well on the most dangerous trip of his life. It occurred in late October of 1978 aboard the *Golden Viking*. Grant was the captain of the eighty-five-foot crab boat as well as a minority owner. With a crew of six, including Phil, Grant had left port in late August.

About two months into the trip, Phil got his hand caught between a line and the hydraulic power block that lifts and lowers crab pots.

The machinery cut off a chunk of his finger, right at the tip, leaving the top of a bone exposed and his nail bent back.

When the injury was stabilized, the *Golden Viking* steamed back to Dutch Harbor, the fishing hub in the Aleutian Islands eight hundred miles southwest of Anchorage, to get Phil proper medical treatment.

Unfortunately, in Dutch Harbor back then, there was no hospital or clinic. An EMT treated Phil's wound preliminarily, but there was only so much he could do without the proper facilities. He put Phil on a flight to Seattle, nearly two thousand miles away, along with a dark prognosis: Phil's finger would likely need to be amputated upon arrival at the hospital there.

Grant was spared the bleak news because, after Phil was dropped off, it was back to the Bering Sea for the *Golden Viking*. That's the hard part of being a captain with a son in the crew. As a father, Grant would have loved to stay behind to be there for Phil. But as a captain, his first obligation was to the ship and its remaining crew.

The *Golden Viking* unloaded its catch at Akutan, a town in the Aleutians East Borough about five hours east of Dutch Harbor, then headed north in search of more crab.

But about a day and a half out of Dutch Harbor, the boat was hit by the tail end of a typhoon.

"The weather conditions were so bad," recalled Grant, "that we stopped for the night because we couldn't see what the sea was doing."

They soon found out in one terrifying instant. The vessel was hit by a gigantic rogue wave that struck with such force that it knocked out windows and filled the wheelhouse with water. The antennas, attached fifty feet above the deck, were knocked off, all the electronic systems fizzled out, and even the compass was torn loose from the wall.

"That wave took everything with it," Grant said.

Such mountains of water are also known as freak waves, monster waves, killer waves, extreme waves, and abnormal waves. Whatever they are called, those large bursts of water, caused by a combination of high winds and strong currents, are the most frightening sight in the sea.

When Grant looked around, he realized the tempered glass in the windows, half an inch or more thick, had not just broken but shattered. The pieces had smashed through the wall behind him, leaving Grant with cuts all over both ears.

The entire chart table, including all the drawers on the bottom, had been blown out into the sea. There was no radio, no radar, no way to determine the ship's immediate surroundings or location, and certainly no way to communicate with the outside world.

"We might as well have been in a canoe out there," Grant said.

As if all that wasn't bad enough, a fire had ignited inside the wall of one of the staterooms, caused when the salt from the seawater shorted some wiring.

The boat's engineer tried to race downstairs to the engine room to pull the breakers on the electrical panel. But with paper and charts from the wheelhouse strewn all over the stairs, he slipped, bounced off a wall, and went tumbling down, step after step, injuring his hip.

The crew managed to extinguish the fire, and Grant and several crew members were able to board up the blasted-out windows by cutting the plywood out of several of the bunks and securing the wood with bolts. With a passable defense against the elements, the boat was in decent shape. It still had power, an adequate supply of food and liquids, and, most important of all, it had Grant, a captain so familiar with that area of the Bering Sea that, to his trained eyes, it was as if there were a highway in front of him with markings as clear as signs leading back to land.

Still, in such uncertain conditions, there is always the danger that the ship will be tossed around so much that even a captain as knowledgeable as Grant could become disoriented.

So he picked up the fallen compass and bolted it to a shelf in the wheelhouse.

"Whether it was right or not, I didn't know," Grant said, "but at least I would know we weren't going around in a circle."

Navigating by the stars wasn't a practical solution because the skies remained overcast much of the time while the storm continued.

"I knew that, as long as I could stay in the direction I was headed," Grant said, "I was eventually going to get to an island, because the Aleutians stretch out over a thousand miles."

While he had a pretty good idea where he was, he had lost all lines of communication to the shore. Back on dry land word soon spread that the *Golden Viking* was missing at sea.

The bad news traveled quickly back to Seattle, where Phil was recovering. Arriving at a Seattle hospital the day after his emergency treatment in Dutch Harbor, he had been assured that amputation was totally unnecessary. The EMT had done such a good job—stitching up Phil's finger and grafting on a piece of skin from his forearm—that the new skin was successfully melding with the old, keeping his finger intact.

Phil was overwhelmed with relief, but the good news was quickly overshadowed when he learned that contact had been lost with the *Golden Viking*. Among the crew of five were not only his dad, but also several others to whom Phil had grown close.

The Coast Guard began a wide search, both by sea and air, but as one day turned into two, then three, four, and five, hope began to fade.

Phil was crushed. The thought of losing his remaining parent was more than he could bear. Still, by then twenty-one years old, he was grudgingly ready to deal with reality. He began to make funeral arrangements for Grant.

Back on the *Golden Viking*, there was no talk of not making it home.

"I wasn't worried about that," said Grant, "as long as we were floating. You can go a long way if you stay above the water."

He had rigged up a method for getting the throttle and steering working, but he still couldn't go much faster than one or two knots.

Slowly, the crippled ship made its way back to Akutan. Not once in that time did Grant see another vessel on the water.

About 6:00 a.m. on Halloween Eve, five days after contact had been lost with Grant's boat, a crewman on a processing ship resting in Akutan Harbor was shaving by a porthole when his eye caught a boat approaching in the distance.

Recognizing it as the *Golden Viking*, the crewman got so excited, he cut himself.

In his typical style, Grant, looking back at the moment, shrugged and said, "They were quite surprised to see me."

"The whole bow was caved in," said Phil. "My dad did a million dollars' worth of damage, but he saved everybody's life."

Grant was still saving lives in his seventies when he was supposed to be retired, though he will never be completely retired as long as he can walk onto a boat.

At age seventy-one, Grant was in his familiar role as a hero on a cod-fishing trip off Unga Island, also in the Aleutians. Joining him on his forty-two-foot fiberglass craft, *The Warrior*, were Phil and Jake.

As the boat headed to nearby Sand Point in choppy seas at the end of their outing to unload their haul, a leak was detected in the hose leading to the oil filter.

While Phil got on the radio to issue a Mayday alert, Grant went down into the engine room with a patch and clamps to cut off the flow of escaping oil. It was the kind of repair job he had been doing for much of his life. Given a little time, he could have done it with his eyes closed.

But he didn't have any time. A strong wind and a fifteen-foot swell were pushing the boat on a collision course with a huge pile of rocks dead ahead.

Because of the angle of the leak, Grant was forced to lean against the engine's exhaust manifold in order to complete his task. The urgency of the moment denied him the opportunity to find a better position.

Without flinching, he focused on patching up the leak, even though his arm was getting burned by the exhaust pipe.

"I'm kvetching," said Jake, recalling the scene, "because I got hot oil sprinkled on my arm while I was holding a flashlight for my grandfather. He had third-degree burns on his arm and he didn't say a fucking word. Four hours later, when all was said and done, he just calmly and quietly peeled his shirt off his arm. The skin was all gone, leaving this huge, raw burned spot. He didn't complain or nothing. I felt like a damn wimp."

When Jake suggested to his grandfather that he get medical treatment for his arm, Grant just shrugged, went to his first aid kit, got out some balm and a bottle of iodine, and that was the end of the conversation.

Grant had repaired the hose with no more than fifty feet separating the boat from the rocks, saving three generations of the Harris family.

To this day, he has a scar down his arm as a reminder of that day, but no regrets about allowing himself to be painfully branded.

"That was a lot better," he says, "than drowning or crashing on those boulders."

A sea captain requires more than bravery and nautical skills. Sometimes patience and determination are also necessary. On one trip in 1964, Grant, with a load of processed crab aboard the *Reefer II*, set out from the south end of Alaska's Kodiak Island bound for Cape Spencer.

That journey across the Gulf of Alaska would normally take two and a half to three days. But because of violent storms that lasted the entire voyage, the boat's journey stretched to eighteen days.

"We weren't sinking or anything," Grant said, "but we were taking on water that whole time. We had the pumps going. If we had sprung a leak, I'm sure we would have sunk."

Barely able to make any headway, the boat limped along.

"We were going just as slow as you could possibly go," Grant said. "It wasn't a good trip."

Grant didn't even need to be at sea to find trouble. Artist Mike Lavallee, a friend of Phil's, noticed something strange about Grant one day in 2010 when he walked into Mike's custom automotive airbrush studio in Snohomish, Washington. Grant's shirt was twisted into a knot centered at chest level.

"Grant, what's going on with your shirt?" Mike wanted to know.

"Well, I almost screwed myself today," he replied.

He meant it literally.

Grant, who likes to do everything for himself, was attaching a shroud to his truck's radiator. Although the protective guard was going to be in the front, he had to stretch his body out and drill a hole from the back end.

Once the electric drill pierced the back side, it came shooting through to the front, emerged, and kept going right into the seventy-seven-year-old Grant.

For an instant, he looked like a man committing suicide by plunging a sword into his midsection.

Fortunately for Grant, the drill stopped just in time. The bit, having enveloped itself in his shirt, came to a halt as it touched the skin in front of his heart. He escaped with nothing worse than a scratch and yet another tale of dodging his demise.

When Mike expressed amazement at how close he had come to sudden death, all Grant said was, "Yep, that's kind of how it goes."

"The Bering Sea never got him," said Mike, "but a drill almost did."

Three centuries separate Vitus Bering and Grant Harris, yet they share a common bond unbroken by time and technology. Both of them sailed the Bering Sea, accepted its frightful challenges, rode its deadly waves, and experienced moments of dread and exhilaration unequaled on any other body of water in the world. And both set a course for future generations. Soon to sail in Grant's wake was Captain Phil Harris, to be followed by Josh and Jake.

CHAPTER 2

LEAST LIKELY TO SUCCEED

"He tried harder than everybody else because he wanted to be accepted."

—*Joe Wabey, Phil's first captain*

Phil Harris had some close friends growing up: Jeff Sheets, Joe Duvey, and Mike Crockett were all constant companions. But there was also another group that Phil spent a lot of time with, though not necessarily by choice: the Bothell Police Department.

When they heard an engine roaring through town at high speed, be it that of a motorcycle or a car, the name Phil Harris usually came to mind.

Grant Harris tried to be a diligent father, but with his wife dead from cancer and his obligations as a carpenter, handyman, and part-time fisherman occupying much of his time, Phil had plenty of opportunities to run wild. And he was about as easy to handle as a bucking bronco.

By the time he was in the seventh grade, Phil had a routine. He'd wait until his father left for work, then grab a couple of pillows, stuff them in the driver's seat of the second family car, and hop in, the added height enabling him to see over the steering wheel.

He didn't get too far because the police also knew his routine. They would pull Phil over and drive him back to his house. Knowing there was no mother at home, the police would then call Grant and tell him, "You can't have your kid out driving around."

Occasionally, if Grant wasn't available, they would take Phil to the police station, where he ended up spending so much time he might as well have been the department mascot.

When Phil turned fifteen, he moved out. He was the drummer in a band that also included Jeff and two other friends, and he decided that he and his fellow musicians needed an apartment where they could live, work on their songs, and entertain the ladies.

Of course, Phil's attendance at school became dismal. But whenever he missed a day, he would simply write a note to explain his absence. They were often long, rambling excuses. After a while, school officials didn't believe a word Phil put down on paper, but what could they do? Since he was living with his friends, there was no adult to verify his claims.

At the end of one semester, out of all his classmates, Phil was voted Least Likely to Succeed after being nominated for that category by a school counselor.

Outwardly, he never seemed to care much about school, treating everything about it with apparent disdain. But deep down, being labeled Least Likely to Succeed cut to his core.

It was a tag he never forgot, even long after he had succeeded beyond the greatest expectations of school officials and the wildest dreams of his classmates.

Where did Phil see himself going after high school? The fishing trips with his father as a youngster had certainly put ideas in his head about a career path. But it wasn't Grant who convinced Phil that fishing was the way to his fortune. It was a classmate.

While Phil was driving around in a beat-up '59 Volkswagen, which he referred to as a "piece of crap," the classmate pulled into the school parking lot every day in a new Chevelle SS.

How did he get that sweet vehicle? His family owned three crab boats.

Phil remembered hearing how a crab fisherman could walk into a bank and get a six-figure unsecured loan because it was assumed he was good for it. That got Phil's attention.

After graduating from high school at sixteen—school officials were no doubt glad to be rid of him—Phil got a job in the fishing industry.

It wasn't catching fish. He wasn't old enough to convince anyone to hire him. But his stepbrother Pat Lamaroux, son of Grant's third wife, Paula, got Phil a job at Pelican Seafoods in Pelican, Alaska, located on the Lisianski Inlet near Juneau.

He worked there for a year, watching with envy as ships would come, unload, and head back out to sea. He desperately wanted to go with them. That was where the adventure and the money lay. But until he was older, all he could do was dream.

In 1974, at the age of seventeen, Phil figured he was ready, but he realized his résumé was lacking a key element: experience. Phil had never been to sea except for those outings with his father as a kid. And that wasn't going to impress anyone.

Still, he was determined to quit Pelican Seafoods, where his job had turned into working as a roofer at the company facility.

When the *American Eagle* crab boat pulled into port, Phil decided this was going to be his ship. Boats were often looking for a greenhorn, the term used for a raw beginner. The only problem was, thirty other guys also had their eyes on the *American Eagle*.

How was Phil going to stand out? Very simple, he thought, after hearing his rivals discussing wages. He would work for free. Who could beat that deal?

"He was this scraggly, long-haired kid, a skinny, unkempt rat," said Joe Wabey, relief skipper on the *American Eagle*. "We weren't even looking to hire anyone, but he was a persistent little prick. Phil hung around the ship and kept bugging us. He kept saying, 'Can I go with you? I got to go with you guys. I don't want to be a cannery worker. I fish. My dad is a fisherman.'"

Seeing that the crew of the *American Eagle* was less than receptive, Phil played his hole card.

"I'll tell you what," he said. "I'll go a whole entire year and you won't have to pay me. I'll go for free."

That got him some attention.

Joe and the other three members of the crew huddled, then gave Phil the thumbs-up.

"Sure," said Joe, who must have looked like a grizzled veteran to Phil, even though Joe was all of twenty-three. "Come on, throw your shit on the boat."

Joe realized this could be a pretty good deal.

"We figured, hell, this will ease our burden a little bit," he later recalled. "We get some free labor out of this guy. And if it doesn't work out, we'll leave him on the beach at Dutch Harbor."

Phil was too elated about getting on a boat to think of the possibility of failure. He rushed to call his dad, anticipating that Grant would be proud.

Worried was more like it. "You might have bit off more than you can chew," Grant told his son. "You get sick on a little boat. And these guys are tough."

Phil also had his doubts, but he hid them well.

Those doubts faded when the boat reached Adak in the Aleutians and Phil found conditions that could not have been better. The sea was calm, the weather tolerable. He sat on a pot and chugged down a beer with a fellow crew member. Life was beautiful.

But not for long.

The next day, the winds started blowing—Phil figured they must have been swirling at 120 miles an hour—and the waves started rising.

He was chopping up herring for bait when the water started pouring across the deck and those old feelings of seasickness overwhelmed him. Now he remembered why he had hated going out with his dad in the beginning.

The greenhorn quickly turned green. Phil crouched on the deck, throwing up until his guts were sore.

It was freezing and the waves kept pounding his body, but he could have put up with all that if only he wasn't so sick.

Pulling himself up, Phil staggered into the galley, where he threw himself across the dinner table and hung on, trying to ride out the waves as if he were on a wild amusement park ride that had to end sometime soon. The captain, Gary Bryant, came in, took one look at Phil, and mockingly told him that he had already predicted this greenhorn wasn't going to make it.

The beach at Dutch Harbor beckoned.

But Phil wouldn't have it. He was hearing "Least Likely to Succeed" all over again. The anger flared, the adrenaline flowed, and the resolve returned.

Not going to make it, eh? We'll see.

With vomit and fish bait dripping from his saturated rain gear, he pulled his shaking body up, steadied his legs as best he could on the bobbing and weaving floor, managed to compose himself enough to give Bryant a defiant glare, and stumbled out into the face of the raging waves to resume his duties.

From that moment of utter vulnerability and failure—spread out on that galley table, a portrait of defeat—Phil Harris, greenhorn, would eventually generate enough will, determination, and work ethic to turn himself into Phil Harris, the fearless captain of *Deadliest Catch*.

But, of course, such a transformation was beyond his comprehension at that moment. All he wanted to do was figure out a way to get through the day. Or even the next hour.

For seven days, try as he did to ignore the seasickness, the frigid weather, and the mountainous waves, Phil couldn't push the thought out of his mind that he might well die, right there on the *American Eagle*.

At first, he didn't get much sympathy from the rest of the crew. They were just as cold, just as wet, and just as susceptible to the dangers of the job as he was, and they weren't complaining.

But beneath their gruff exteriors, crew members gradually felt some admiration for the wide-eyed, eager kid. "There was something likable about the guy," said Joe. "You've got to admire somebody with that much persistence. He tried so hard that he was almost a nuisance. You're working and you've got this little puppy dog following you around, two steps behind you.

"He had a lot to learn and he was a slow learner, but we kept giving him opportunities. We broke him in right. Phil didn't need bossing around because he was willing to work. If you told him to do something, he would do it."

And what the crew told Phil to do were the things nobody else wanted to do.

"We gave him all the shit work," said Joe. "His number-one job was to chop bait. He would sit there all day and do that, and never complain."

Nobody else complained about Phil, just as long as they didn't have to share a bunk with him. He had a problem with personal hygiene, and while it's not as if any of the other crew members looked as if they were going to the school prom, Phil was particularly grungy.

"He was always dirty," said Joe. "He never washed. He was filthy. I don't even think he brushed his teeth."

His nickname became Dirt.

That name stuck like the substance itself. Thirty years later, Joe would still greet Phil with, "Hey, Dirt."

Phil didn't care what they called him on the *American Eagle* as long as they kept him on board.

"His attitude was his greatest asset," said Joe. "He was always fun, never down, even if he had his face in the dirt all day. He always kept everybody laughing."

But it wasn't always easy for Phil to laugh along with them, because he was the number-one target of crewmembers' pranks. That was a given, a rite of passage that must be endured by all greenhorns. But in Phil's case, one prank went over the line, even for a crab boat.

"The thing about practical jokes on a boat," said Joe, "is that they tend to escalate. Each guy tries to outdo the next. With Phil, it ended up with us taking a live, forty-pound octopus and putting it in his bunk. We then covered it up with his blanket."

Even happy-go-lucky Phil didn't laugh that one off. "That was the last straw," Joe admitted, "because that octopus made a mess. After that, we decided that maybe the bunks should be sacred. Practical jokes were fine everywhere else, but you've got to have a place to sleep."

Phil knew that, for the foreseeable future, he would be stuck on the receiving end of every prank. Considering his status at that point, he didn't dare go after any other crew member.

"He knew he was on thin ice," said Joe. "We could let him go in a heartbeat."

After a couple of months of watching Phil do the grunt work day after day and remembering he was doing this for nothing, crew members began to ease his burden.

"You kind of felt bad for the guy," Joe said. Bad enough that crew members began slipping Phil food known to settle the stomach and money out of their pockets. It was only walk-around money, a couple hundred bucks, but that all changed when one of the crew members got hurt. Needing a quick replacement and with no other options, they went to the only other person on board, the greenhorn.

With the benefit of the harsh lessons he had learned over the previous few months, Phil proved ready for the promotion.

By the time the season was over, he was a full-fledged crab fisherman, earning the same share of the revenue as everybody else, $120,000.

Putting $120,000 in the hands of any seventeen-year-old would be a questionable move. Putting it in the hands of a wild kid like Phil could have been downright disastrous.

But when he came home to Bothell, his first thought wasn't drugs and alcohol. That would come later. Phil's first desire was for vindication. He just couldn't shake that label that had been put on his head, "Least Likely to Succeed."

The female counselor who had nominated him for that embarrassing category lived in the neighborhood where Phil had grown up. Driving down the block, he saw a for-sale sign in front of her house. Asking price: $38,000.

He deposited his $120,000 check in a nearby bank, then asked for $40,000 back in cash.

Phil was told he could get a cashier's check for that amount.

Nope, he insisted, I want it in cash. In a paper bag.

Soon, there was a knock on the door of the counselor's home. When her husband answered it, Phil barged right past him, paper bag in hand, marched into the kitchen, and dumped the cash on the table.

Amazed, the couple were also defiant. They told Phil to take his $40,000 and leave. They weren't interested in selling the house to him.

That was fine with Phil; he wasn't really interested in buying it. He just wanted to show the counselor that he had succeeded after all.

That moment of satisfaction, however, wasn't enough to prevent a lifetime of insecurity. That label of derision stuck in his head until the day he died.

In later years, Phil admitted that, despite all his success, he never felt he was equal to his rival captains, always believing he was an inferior fisherman, always the greenhorn, the seventeen-year-old on the *American Eagle* who was treated with such disdain. As a result, Phil decided that he had to be the hardest worker, the last one to head for port after all the other ships had set a course for home.

By the following year, with Bryant gone and Joe promoted to captain, Phil was hired by the *American Eagle* to be part of a three-man crew. That should have been a boost to his ego.

"When you a hire a guy, he has to be pretty exceptional," said Joe, "because, with only three crew members on deck, you can't have a bad guy. It just doesn't work. There's no cushion, no margin for putting up with a slacker. Efficiency is the key with three men. But I felt Phil could handle it because, by then, he had earned our respect."

Phil's reputation as a competent fisherman grew in his second season aboard the *American Eagle*, but the respect he had gained was not unconditional as he learned the following season when he was given the responsibility of manning the wheelhouse at night while the rest of the crew slept.

"When you start out on a boat," Joe said, "you normally move up to higher and higher levels of duty. Putting a guy on wheel watch means moving him to the pinnacle of trust. You ease someone into it, starting him out when there is still daylight."

When Phil was promoted by Joe, it was back in the seventies when wheelhouses weren't equipped with all the electronic backup systems built in today.

"We didn't have the watch alarms and the monitoring equipment," Joe said. "You have to have a lot of trust in the guy you put up there, trust that he's going to check the machinery when he's supposed to, run the course properly, watch for traffic, and not run over buoys."

One night, after the *American Eagle* had left Dutch Harbor and was heading east through Unimak Pass, Joe put Phil, who had worked day watch, on his first night shift, a two- to three-hour session.

"Everybody who is sleeping," Joe said, "trusts you to do the right thing."

Interaction with foreign ships, some four hundred to five hundred feet long, the majority Japanese or Korean, began quickly after leaving port. While communication with those ships is relatively good these days, back then, there was little if any talk back and forth. Most of the operators of the foreign ships, unable to speak English, would simply ignore any transmission from a U.S. boat.

Phil's job in the wheelhouse that night was to make sure the *American Eagle* made it safely through Unimak Pass, a section of the Bering Sea that sometimes looked like rush hour on a downtown U.S. freeway, with container ships, fishing vessels, and all sorts of craft plying the waters. The good news was, there was good visibility for Phil's first watch after dark.

"It was crystal clear that night," Joe recalled. "Flat calm. All Phil had to do was drive straight and avoid traffic."

Joe didn't feel fully comfortable leaving Phil, who was still only twenty, up there alone. Nevertheless, Joe went down to his bunk to grab a few hours of sleep. He couldn't turn off his mind, though. He kept thinking about what could go wrong in the wheelhouse.

Finally, his concerns overwhelmed his tiredness. "I come upstairs," Joe said, "walk into the wheelhouse, and there is Phil, sitting in the captain's chair with his hooded sweatshirt pulled over his head. He was slouched down so low, I couldn't even say for sure that there was anybody in the chair.

"When I spun the chair around, there was Phil, dead asleep."

What really sent a shiver through Joe was what he saw behind him in the boat's wake.

"We had just come through a fleet of about fifteen big trawlers that were now about three or four miles behind us," Joe said. "He had not even altered course.

"I thought, Oh my God, are you kidding me?"

Joe exploded. Phil awakened to the sounds of his infuriated boss yelling in his ear, telling him in very clear, descriptive language that he had endangered the lives of every crew member.

"I tried him, but it didn't work out," said Joe. "It could have been disastrous, but at least he learned his lesson.

"Still, I never gave him that watch again, never put him in the wheelhouse in Unimak Pass."

CHAPTER 3

DRINKIN', DRUGGIN', RIDIN'

My dad once told me that when he was a young crab fisherman, he'd get a big, fat paycheck, buy huge amounts of cocaine, stash it all in a shoe box, rent the penthouse of a nice hotel, and rotate the girls in and out. That's how he lived his life for a long time. He'd get a check for $80,000, but, after three weeks, it was gone. That's what crab fishermen did in those days. There was no shame to the game.

—Josh

Whether he was out in the precarious Bering Sea or back in the familiar surroundings of Bothell, Phil Harris was never far from a party. And most of the time, it was his party.

His wild days and nights, both in Dutch Harbor and on the back roads of Bothell, are legendary. "When we came in with a load of crab to the cannery," said Joe Wabey, Phil's first captain, "it would take two days to off-load it. That gave us two days to drink, party, sleep, and party some more while also getting in a few boat chores.

"Phil was a colorful guy, huge when it came to partying back when he was one of my crew members, but he sure had the ugliest girlfriends I've ever seen. He would hook up with the cannery girls—I guess we all did in those days—but his girls were distinctive. There was one we called Fish Face because her eyes were out to the side of her head and she was kind of grey in color. He had another one that looked like the old greasy-haired rocker, Patti Smith, but she was really nice, the nicest of the group."

Phil fit right in with the wild bunch that walked the streets, caroused in the bars, and worked the docks of Dutch Harbor, a port within the city limits of Unalaska, population 4,376. Dutch Harbor is a focal point for commercial fishermen, seafood processors, and all sorts of boat operators.

Vessels badly damaged by the ravages of the Bering Sea usually wind up in that harbor, designated a port of refuge by both the state and federal governments.

Thousands of ships enter Dutch Harbor brimming with fish that is soon shipped all over the world, reaching markets in North America, Europe, and the Far East. For the last twenty-two years, Dutch Harbor has led the nation in seafood exports, handling almost 1 million tons of seafood annually.

Just getting there is an adventure. Fishing in the Bering Sea is like a dip in a wading pool compared to the danger of landing at Dutch Harbor Airport. It's like trying to touch down on a large life raft, the uninviting waters of the sea waiting on either end of the runway for any plane that misses its target. Compounding the problem are sometimes-ferocious winds and the ever-unpredictable storms.

When first-time visitors ask if they can fly out on a specific day, they are told, "Nobody can be certain of leaving Dutch Harbor when they want. They leave when they can."

Danger has long haunted this town. A century ago, an epidemic of Spanish flu decimated the population. In 1942 in the midst of World War II, Dutch Harbor, site of a U.S. naval air station and army barracks, was bombed by twenty-five Japanese fighter planes in a two-day battle that left forty-three American servicemen dead, and a ship, oil tanks, barracks, and warehouses damaged or destroyed.

Today, bald eagles, drunks, and a vampire are the biggest threats to the population. The vampire was a local who, according to the *Los*

Angeles Times, was found with blood all over him, wandering around town on his bike, claiming his ex-girlfriend had turned him into a bloodsucker.

The Unisea bar, advertised as the spot "Where Fish and Drink Become One," is packed with crazy characters looking for a few hours of relief after weeks at sea. On any given night, many in there look like a cross between Jack Sparrow and Long John Silver.

And right in the middle of it for thirty-five years was Phil, his gravelly voice, bleary-eyed look, and distinctively tattooed arms standing out even in that crowd.

"He was definitely rough around the edges," said Keith Colburn, captain of the *Wizard*. "There were guys in the fleet who were strait-laced and operated by the book. They were superprofessional mariners. You'd never see those guys in a bar. They were there for a reason, and that reason was business.

"Phil knew how to mix business with pleasure. He understood that sometimes you've got to have a good time to handle what you are going to be dealing with. He'd be in the bars throwing the drinks back, trying to stay loose because he knew, once he got ready to leave the harbor, he was going to be an absolute nervous wreck. Once he left the dock, the fun time stopped.

"Going into a crab season, you are about as tense as you can get. It's like a game seven of the NBA playoffs. You've got maybe four days to fish and, if you fuck up, you are going to be screwed. But, if you land on the crab, you are going to be a hero."

To Colburn, Phil was a hero. "There were hooligans and bums in the fleet," he said, "even pirates and crooks. Phil was nowhere near those guys. He was a class act."

Sig Hansen, captain of the *Northwestern*, said Phil took a unique approach to the pursuit of happiness from the moment his boat docked in Dutch Harbor. "For the rest of us, the routine was standard," Hansen said. "You live on your boat, you go out and party, and then you come back to your boat.

"Not Phil. He'd get a room at a hotel on shore. He had that style, that coolness. He'd say, 'I don't want to have to worry about crawling back to the boat if I've had too much to drink. I'll crawl back to my room.'"

Hansen thought it was such a great idea that he started to get a room for himself when coming into Dutch Harbor. "I didn't do it in the beginning because I'm too damn cheap," Hansen conceded, "and I thought it made you look like you were just trying to be a big shot.

"But I came to realize that Phil was right. So you spend a hundred dollars for the night if you're going to go out and act goofy, and then you don't have to worry about getting back to the dock. You just have to get to your hotel bed. That's more civilized."

While the comforts of a soft bed might still be appealing, having a private party headquarters is no longer as practical.

"It's all different now," said Joe. "It only takes about eighteen hours to off-load and you're back out again, so that has cut way down on the partying."

There was no such thing as cutting down on the partying when Phil would return to Bothell after a fishing trip.

"When Phil came home," said his longtime friend Jeff Sheets, "he'd call me immediately. It was usually about four in the morning. I'd pick up the phone and I'd hear the voice on the other end say, 'Get over here. I'm back.' My wife would chew me out as I got dressed because she knew I wasn't going to work that day.

"By the time I got over to Phil's place, he had already gotten a quarter ounce of coke and a couple of bottles of Stoli vodka."

Joe Duvey, another Bothell friend, said the routine was always the same throughout the 1970s and much of the 1980s: "Drinkin', druggin', and ridin' bikes. That was about it."

Once he became established as a crab boat captain, Phil had plenty of money to spend on toys. For him, the toys consisted of Corvettes, Harleys, and a Porsche, his wild rides in the driver's seat fueled by drugs and alcohol. It was never boring when Phil was in town. "Total chaos was more like it," Joe said. Sit around with the Bothell gang today and the tales from the old days never seem to end.

"One night," Joe said, "Phil was riding one of his bikes, the beautiful, supercustom one. Hauling ass with a couple of other guys, he went off the road."

Phil went flying into some bushes, winding up scratched and bruised. But where was his motorcycle? Lying flat on his back, Phil spotted it.

Directly overhead. It had soared twenty feet into the air and come to rest upside down in a tree.

"The guys he was with came back and helped him drag the bike down," Joe said, "but one wheel was bent."

Phil tried to straighten it out by bashing it with a tree branch. But when he got back on the bike and attempted to ride it, the cycle weaved all over the road, that wheel far from functional.

"Many of his evenings were like that," Joe said. "They would start out all right and then he would do something crazy."

Jeff remembered another disastrous outing with that same bike: "Phil was coming down the hill on the way to his house," Jeff said, "and he tried to put on the brakes, but nothing happened. He ended up riding up the side of the house of his next-door neighbor, Hugh Gerrard. The bike flipped over and flattened Phil."

Even starting his bike could be a hazardous task for Phil. "He would put gas directly into the carburetor," Joe said. "It would always backfire. I'm surprised it never burned up in all the thousands of times he did that. He would just fire it up and off he'd go."

Phil was never shy about drawing attention to himself. If he was in Bothell on the Fourth of July, it was guaranteed that he would be crouched over a crate or two of outlawed but state-of-the-art pyrotechnics. He could put on a fireworks show as bright and explosive as any in the country.

None of Phil's wild antics as an adult surprised the folks in Bothell. They'd been seeing his act since he was a teenager. Back then, he had an old hot rod that he kept in the backyard of his father's house. Grant put the vehicle up on blocks because he didn't want Phil driving it. With someone as rebellious as his son, Grant might as well have hung a sign on the car that read "Drive me."

Phil and Jeff would sneak over there at night, bolt a set of tires on the hot rod, slip it out of the yard, and race it past Bothell's city hall, burning rubber, the screeching sounds and distinctive smell awakening anybody within a block of the midnight mischief makers.

Then they would peel out of there, head back to Grant's house, and try to be as quiet as possible in returning the car to the blocks.

"It wouldn't be long before the Bothell cops came shining their lights," Jeff said. "They knew it was us. They could see the tire marks going into the backyard."

One time, Phil woke up in the middle of the night craving booze, but there wasn't any in his house. The nearest liquor store was three miles away. He still had that car sitting on the blocks, but at that point it would only go in reverse. So, naturally, Phil got it off the blocks and drove three miles backward to satisfy his craving.

Grant wasn't happy about Phil's late night joyrides or having the police prowling through his yard, but he was even more agitated when the teenaged Phil borrowed a motor Grant kept in his garage and it wound up at the bottom of the slough that runs through downtown Bothell.

Phil didn't have mischief in his mind when he and Jeff took the motor. They just wanted it to power a ten-foot mahogany boat Phil had bought.

Seemed innocent enough.

Phil was able to get the boat up to about thirty miles an hour. After he took a run with it, it was Jeff's turn.

"I was just passing the bridge in downtown Bothell," Jeff said, "when, all of a sudden, I'm staring at a flock of ducks directly ahead.

Bam, I hit them, causing a hole to pop open in the bottom of the boat. Down she goes, with Grant's motor.

"The hardest part was going to his house to explain to him how his motor wound up on a sunken boat."

Phil's most infamous Bothell exploits always seemed to involve the police, whether he was on their side or in their face.

On one occasion when he was well into adulthood, he drove his orange Corvette, a 1972 model in pristine condition with a tan interior, over to visit the owner of a gas station where he had worked while in high school.

As the two stood talking, a teenager snuck into the Corvette and took off.

While the gas-station owner called the police, Phil jumped into another of his cars, a Porsche parked nearby, and roared off in pursuit of his beloved Corvette.

The police were soon fully engaged in the chase, but not as engaged as Phil.

Heading northeast out of Bothell, the car thief was about four or five miles into his joyride when he looked in his rearview mirror.

There's no way to determine his precise reaction, but it's safe to assume he did a double take. Yes, the police were hot on his trail, but so was Phil, who had somehow managed to get ahead of the cops.

What could be more frightening than seeing Phil Harris, hair flying, murder in his eyes, bearing down on you?

Perhaps a distraction like that contributed to what happened next. Or maybe it was just the fact that, at the speed he was traveling, the thief wasn't able to handle the ninety-degree turn in the road.

Whatever the reason, with Phil helpless to do anything about it, his treasured Corvette missed the turn and crashed into a telephone pole.

"It almost broke the car in half," said Jeff.

"I was ready to kill that kid," Phil later told Joe, "but the cops pulled me off."

Was the teenager seriously hurt?

"Hopefully, but I don't know," said Joe. "We never asked."

On another occasion, Phil and his Porsche went from pursuer to pursuee. It occurred on a highway about fifty miles south of Seattle.

Heading north, Phil pulled even with a cop, stared at him, then, for no obvious reason, flipped him off and floored it.

To Phil, flooring it meant reaching speeds well in excess of a hundred miles an hour.

"From what I heard," said Joe, "he was really cooking."

As he approached Bothell, Phil could see traffic had slowed to a crawl. He wasn't particularly concerned, because there were no longer any police behind him.

Must be an accident, he figured.

But as Phil inched along, he could see that the delay was being caused by a roadblock up ahead. As he got closer, he realized there was a contingent of heavily armed police checking each vehicle.

They had been letting the cars ahead of him pass unimpeded, but once they spotted Phil and the Porsche, the police zeroed in on him and jerked him out of the car.

"Turns out they were looking for me," Phil later told Joe. "I had forgotten all about it."

A furious search of Phil's car ensued, from top to bottom, but when the police, who were very familiar with his antics, couldn't find anything, and an attorney intervened, claiming Phil's rights were being violated, he got off with just a ticket and a stiff fine. In any other city, he'd have wound up wearing an orange jumpsuit.

Phil loved nothing more than to roar through Bothell at a breakneck pace, but his fellow travelers weren't always up to his speed. After Phil dropped a small fortune on a new Corvette, he asked his friend Dan Mittman to take care of it while he chased crab.

When Phil returned from the sea, he was delighted to see that his car was in perfect condition. But he was also puzzled.

"Hey, this car only has two-tenths of a mile added on since I left," said Phil, his eyebrows raised.

"You were gone three months," Dan told him, "and in that time, I moved the car around to avoid any sun spotting or tire rot. Two-tenths of a mile was precisely what was required to do the job."

"I'm not tripping 'cause you only moved the car two-tenths of a mile," said Phil, his voice starting to rise. "I'm telling you, that damned car is like a fuckin' thoroughbred and has to be driven, and driven hard."

Phil's friends appreciated the much-needed reprieve provided by his return trips to Alaska. It allowed them a chance to calm down from the high-octane surge he injected into their everyday lives. Running with him was exhilarating, but it sure wore a body out.

Teenager or adult, Dutch Harbor or Bothell, Phil himself never seemed to slow down. Until he reached his fifties and his body finally rebelled, he remained an oversized kid, Peter Pan with tattoos.

CHAPTER 4

CAPTAIN KID

When I was just a deckhand, wet and freezing my ass off, I'd look up at the wheelhouse and see the captain up there, all dry and warm, wearing slippers. I wanted to be the one wearing slippers.

—Phil

Despite all the wild times on shore, when Phil was on the high seas, he was all business. It was sometimes hard to believe he was the same person. But once his boat left the dock, the drunken, drugged-out partier became a responsible, hardworking, no-nonsense fisherman.

He fell asleep on Joe Wabey that one time, but never again. Wabey's anger awakened Phil to the demands of the job, but what really inspired him was Joe's work ethic.

Joe never asked his crew to do anything he wouldn't do himself. While fishing, Joe would average only one hour of sleep a night. He once went seven days without shutting his eyes.

"You learn to function," Joe said. "I enjoyed fishing. I liked the thrill of it. And when you're running a three-man crew, who is going to take your place? I didn't want to stop. I wanted to fill the boat up with crab and get back.

"Normally, we'd work anywhere from twenty-four to seventy-two hours and then take a break."

A break meant getting a few hours' sleep, and then it was back to fishing.

"That's not a normal schedule," Joe conceded. "I was kind of the extreme when it came to captains. At least I was told that. A lot of the people who worked for me over the years said I was the hardest skipper they ever had. Most of the time, they didn't say that in such nice terms."

Phil wasn't intimidated by Joe's demanding schedule. He was challenged.

"I think Phil tried to compete with me, outwork me," said Joe. "He couldn't keep up, but he put in some long hours. I think he got his work ethic from me.

"He was a good fisherman. I really came to respect him for that."

That respect was especially meaningful for Phil coming from someone like Joe who knew as well as anyone how difficult it is to master crab fishing.

The success of any hunter depends on the depth of his or her knowledge of the history, location, tendencies, strengths, and weaknesses of the quarry being sought.

So it is with crab fishermen. Beneath the bravado and tough exterior, these are calculating professionals with a deep understanding of the creatures they pursue below the surface of the sea.

"There is a lot to learn and you can't get it from a book, a video, or even by watching *Deadliest Catch*," said Josh. "Like our dad before us, Jake and I have soaked up the knowledge we need to do the job—everything from the nature of crabs to the operation of the boat—in the middle of the Bering Sea."

There are five primary types of crab caught in the Bering Sea—red king, blue king, golden king, bairdi, and opilio snow crab. Although the seasons have varied somewhat over the decades based on weather and migration patterns, the year generally begins with the hunt for opilio in January, and bairdi in winter and spring, shifting to golden king in late summer, then red and blue in fall.

Crabs have five pairs of limbs. Four pairs serve as legs, allowing the crab to walk along the ocean floor, while the front pair, called che-lipeds, are claws that function like arms. The crab uses them for hold-ing or carrying food, cracking shells, digging, or attempting to ward off obstacles and potentially hostile life forms. If a crab loses a leg, it has the ability to regrow it.

A red king crab can travel up to one mile per day on those legs and up to one hundred miles a year in order to migrate.

A crab's outer shell, called the carapace or exoskeleton, does not grow along with the crab. Therefore, as it increases in size, the crab must shed the shell, a process called molting. In preparation, it reab-sorbs calcium carbonate from the old shell, secreting enzymes and ab-sorbing seawater to aid the process. The crab backs out of its shell, also leaving behind its esophagus, stomach lining, and part of its intestine. It secretes calcium to create a new shell that hardens over a few weeks. Crabs molt fifteen to twenty times during their lives.

Some crabs live ten to twenty years and weigh an average of six to ten pounds, but some grow in excess of twenty pounds. The world rec-ord belongs to a red king crab caught in the northern Pacific Ocean that weighed 33.1 pounds.

In his early years aboard the *American Eagle*, Phil learned many les-sons, some harder than others. One of the toughest came in his first year on the boat. He was being taught how to operate the crane that lifts the eight-hundred-pound cages—or pots as they are commonly called—used to catch crabs.

"It takes a little bit of finesse to work that crane," Joe said.

On deck, the pots are stacked and tied tightly together until they are needed. On that particular day, they were piled high in the stern.

Phil was being instructed on how to lift one of those pots in the grasp of the crane, but he could only get it to rise a couple of feet be-fore the crane stalled. Phil soon discovered the problem: there was one line still keeping that pot tethered to the stack.

A crewman named Bob Mason, armed with a knife on the end of

a stick, climbed up on an adjoining stack to cut the line, but it was just out of reach, the stick a little too short. So Mason got on his stomach and stretched his body down in order to sever that final restraint.

At that instant, Phil eased up on the crane, and the pot came hurtling down. "I don't know if he had a brain fart or what," said Joe. The eight-hundred-pound pot came crashing down on Mason's head, squeezing it between two stacks.

"Fortunately, he was wearing a leather flier's cap with earflaps," said Joe, "but still, that pot almost took his ears off. He was bleeding from both of them."

Joe and the other crew members lifted the pot off Mason and gently lowered him to the deck.

"Phil was beside himself," Joe said.

"Oh my God, oh my God," Phil shrieked to no one in particular. "What have I done?"

Mason had suffered a skull fracture and was taken to a nearby clinic, then flown out to a fully equipped hospital. Although Mason survived, no one on the *American Eagle* ever saw him again.

Neither Joe nor the rest of the crew criticized Phil for what had happened. "He felt bad enough already," said Joe.

Phil stayed on the *American Eagle* for nearly four years. As he gained experience and confidence, his desire to be more than a deckhand grew.

He could see, however, that his dream would never be fulfilled on the *American Eagle*. "I certainly wasn't going to let go of the throttle and turn the boat over to him," Joe said. "He had higher aspirations than working for me, and I could certainly understand that."

But opportunity beckoned elsewhere. Phil's father, Grant, an engineer on the *Golden Viking* at the time, had accepted an offer to buy a piece of that crab boat and become its captain in 1976.

Grant assured Phil that, if he joined him, he would soon make that coveted climb to the wheelhouse to be the relief skipper.

So in 1977, Phil said farewell to the only crab boat he'd ever known and joined his father who, a year later, let him live his dream by taking command of a boat.

Grant didn't make Phil the relief captain just because he was trying to further his son's career, although that was certainly on Grant's mind. He wouldn't have allowed Phil to become a captain if he didn't think his son could handle it. Not with the lives of the crew dependent on the competence of the man in charge of the boat.

"As a matter of fact," said Grant, "Phil was a much better fisherman than I was."

"Phil was ready when he went over to the *Golden Viking*," said Joe. "I knew he'd become a captain because he had more drive than Grant. I don't mean any disrespect for Grant, but he was more of a gentleman fisherman.

"If Phil had stayed on the *American Eagle*, he might have wound up like some of the crew members that were there fifteen, twenty years and never advanced."

While he advanced quickly, Phil's quick promotion to relief captain didn't go over so well with some of the deckhands.

"He went from bait man to the wheelhouse really quickly," said Tony Lara, who would later be Phil's relief skipper on the *Cornelia Marie*. "But it took him twenty years to earn the respect of the industry. He sat in the wheelhouse chair in his early twenties, but he certainly wasn't the best back then. He wasn't the fisherman he later became. He didn't have the esteem of his peers. That's because he was the kid whose father was captain and part owner of the boat, and so he was given a shortcut to the wheelhouse. That's two strikes against you right there."

Deckhands would walk by, muttering, 'The only reason he's sitting in that big chair is because of his old man.'"

Sensitive to the feelings of the crew and realizing that if Grant stuck up for Phil he would lack credibility because of their relationship, Reidar Tynes, one of the major owners of the *Golden Viking*, stepped in and told the disgruntled deckhands, "We're giving this kid the boat because we think he can do it. You guys have been with us a lot of years, so please, help him in any way you can."

Tynes had sought to give the crew an olive branch. But any goodwill he created was squandered by Phil on his first trip back into Dutch Harbor as captain. Entering the port, a boat must make a sharp right turn to reach the cannery. The young Phil miscalculated and tipped the *Golden Viking* over on its side.

He was able to right it without causing any injuries or major damage to the boat, but the same could not be said for his image. Phil later admitted he was terribly embarrassed by not only looking to his crew like an inept greenhorn behind the wheel, but by doing so in full view of all the other captains docked in Dutch.

He was never again responsible for such a glaring accident. And motivated by his early screwups, Phil went on to establish his skill as a fisherman and build a solid reputation as a crab boat captain.

Phil was coming of age at just the right time. The opportunities for success in the crab fishing industry were never better than in the golden era of the mid-1970s.

In the early twentieth century, the hunt for crab had become popular, but the technology to make it highly lucrative was still decades away. There were no sophisticated computers to chart courses, no eight-hundred-pound pots to catch crab because there was no hydraulic system to lift those pots in and out of the water, and no high-powered lights to make night fishing possible. Fishermen would go out in smaller boats, converted trawlers that didn't even have holding tanks to keep the crab alive.

"Those boats weren't designed to do what our boats do today," said Sig Hansen, captain of the *Northwestern*. "They were junk."

Without the proper vessels, most of the Bering Sea was off-limits. "Back in the late fifties and sixties, they would just fish along the Aleutian Islands," said Sig, whose father, Sverre, was a captain in that era.

Back then, with radar as the primary locating device, the fishermen would triangulate their fishing spots at sea by using landmarks on the islands that could be seen from their boats.

"It was a pain in the ass," said Sig, "like fishing in the blind."

They may have lacked the tools of today's crab fishermen, but the older generation could certainly match the current group when it came to colorful characters. The old-timers could have put on a *Deadliest Catch* series every bit as entertaining as today's shows, and Sverre was as colorful as any of them. When he was young, Sig used to hear a story about how his father's boat sprang a leak while Sverre was cooking steaks. His father looked at the water gathering on the deck but also kept an eye on his steak.

"I'm not going on an empty stomach," he proclaimed to his deck-hands.

By the early 1970s, the boats had grown bigger and the technology had improved, allowing the vessels to roam much farther from shore. No longer did they need island landmarks to guide them.

But the single biggest factor in growing the industry was the addition of sodium lights, generating beams powerful enough to illuminate the search for crab regardless of the time and circumstances.

In January in the Bering Sea, the sun doesn't come up until around ten in the morning and is gone by four in the afternoon. Add in the dim daylight hours on sunless or stormy days and the dark waters of the Bering Sea, and the working hours and conditions for crab fishermen were extremely limited.

"The sodium lights changed everything," said Sig. "Now fishing at night was possible. You could fish twenty-four hours a day. And you could venture farther out and not worry about getting stuck out there in the dark if you had problems."

The result was the heyday of crab fishing, beginning around 1974. By 1978, when Grant allowed Phil to take a turn commanding the *Golden Viking*, the business was really booming.

"Phil was part of the generation," said Sig, "who got in at the peak."

CHAPTER 5

BEAUTY AND THE PIRATE

I probably knew Phil better than anyone.

On the plus side, he was confident, gutsy, a thrill seeker, persistent, adventurous, a take-charge type, full of energy, fun, exciting, generous, extravagant, first class, yet casual, kind, a good provider, sympathetic, humorous, good-natured, very forgiving, an animal lover, and almost always upbeat.

I admired his strength and how hard he worked. I had no idea just how hard until I watched *Deadliest Catch*. I am sorry for all the times I yelled at him when he'd call from the boat, especially during a bad storm, to say he loved me and the kids. I wonder if it wasn't because he thought he might not make it back.

On the downside, he could be loud, bossy, restless, fidgety, reckless, out of control, lawless, a showoff, boastful, disorganized, messy, foulmouthed, arrogant, self-centered, egotistical, stubborn, overly indulgent, an excessive drinker, a five-pack-a-day smoker, a drug user, gambler, and womanizer. He was a very addictive person, someone who just couldn't do anything in moderation.

Yet when I think of him now, I see my knight in shining armor.

—*Mary Harris*

The hot-pink neon sign flickered atop the old building in Woodinville, Washington. Jagged cracks snaked across the sign's glass surface, and some of its letters were only partially illuminated. But that was no problem for the unruly horde of fishermen, loggers, and construction workers descending on Goodtime Charley's on that April night in 1978. They didn't need a compass to find their destination. Brazen men such as these were drawn to strip joints like fish to bait.

At least one police officer suspected that the good times involved more than just stripping. Officers saw fancy cars belonging to suspected pimps regularly drop off and pick up women. Often, officers were required to do more than just watch the scene from a distance. "I remember going to calls there for fights between patrons and employees," King County police sergeant Rick Krogh told the *Seattle Times*.

Inside the topless go-go bar, the cigarette haze was thick, swirling along as though fueled by the loud disco music pulsating throughout the nightspot. A voluptuous dancer named Holly McMillan, stage name Heartbreakin' Holly, worked the boisterous crowd.

The fishermen filled every corner of the room, behaving as if they owned the place. Which in effect they did, considering how much of their cash they left there nightly.

After her set, Holly pulled aside a fellow dancer, Mary Smith, a willowy twenty-three-year-old creature with raven hair down to her knees. The genes from a French father and Chinese/Polynesian mother had combined to give Mary delicate features and an exotic vibe that would have stood out in any club, but especially in this low-brow establishment.

Holly pointed out a rough customer to Mary, one whose ruggedness wore well on him.

"That guy really wants to meet you," Holly said. "He's in love with you." Mary rolled her eyes, but Holly would not let up.

"I told him you were married," Holly said. "He said, 'Oh bummer, is she happily married?' I said, 'No, I think she's getting a divorce.' He said, 'Great. Better yet.'"

Mary had been a waitress at Goodtime Charley's for three and a half years, serving beer and food. Mostly beer. She knew the customers would drink vinegar and chew on newspapers as long as they could ogle beautiful, sexy women. And she knew how big the wads of money were that the clientele tossed onto the stage or stuffed into the skimpy outfits of Goodtime Charley's fantasy females.

Still, Mary's shyness and lack of confidence kept her off the dance floor. "I was scared to death to go out there," she said.

She finally made the big leap into the spotlight after a particularly traumatic night in her ever rockier marriage. Her husband, who, according to Mary, abused her in the past, had locked her in the bathroom and refused to let her out to go to work.

It was a busy night at Goodtime Charley's, wall-to-wall customers packing the joint.

Where was Mary? When the club's manager, John Lewis, called her, she explained the problem. No excuse. Lewis sent the club bouncer, a man named Tiny, who was anything but, to Mary's house. Imposing and distinctive, with a muscular frame, shiny bald head, and one sparkling earring, Tiny didn't look like a man who would shy away from a confrontation. Mary's husband wasn't about to test him as Tiny escorted Mary out the door.

She knew that night that she couldn't go on like that. She was going to have to save up enough money to move out. And the only way to do that was to put down her drink tray and put on her dancing shoes.

Though her confidence grew as she demonstrated her ability on her feet, and she was happy to be free of waiting on drunks, she still hated the obligation to strut and grind night after night. But she stuck to it tenaciously, and, in just three months, Mary saved enough money to carve out an independent life for her and her two kids.

"He's got a lot of money!" Holly whispered as Mary strolled over to the mystery man.

"So what? It's not like he's going to give it to me," Mary yelled back.

Mary sized the stranger up. A fisherman. Fresh off the boat. He had that Kurt Cobain grunge look about him. His outdated bell-bottom jeans were liberally sprinkled with holes. He wore a dirty down vest, a shabby plaid shirt, and sported stringy, oily, dishwater-blond hair under a knit cap. He was over six feet tall, but skinny as a rail at about 160 pounds.

Close up, she caught an acrid whiff from this lanky but strangely charismatic bad boy. Phew! Mary recognized the funk of sour seafood that branded working fishermen. She didn't have to ask where this guy had been.

Nevertheless, Mary flashed an ivory smile and asked him if he wanted a dance. He introduced himself as Phil Harris and told her he wasn't interested in a dance. "I'm interested in you," he informed her bluntly. "Want to go for a drink when you get off work?"

Mary explained that she wasn't interested in starting up with a youngster. Phil, all of twenty-one years old, lied, saying he was twenty-four.

That's when she first noticed his eyes. They were a striking baby blue and danced with a confidence unexpected from someone in his early twenties.

Another thing that struck Mary was the obeisance being paid Phil by the seamen he had come in with. They eagerly jumped at his every command.

"Get me a beer." "Go find me a pack of smokes." They did whatever he said. Mary thought the interplay was hilarious. She wondered what they would do if he told them to go take a piss for him.

Phil explained that he was a crab boat captain, skippering the *Golden Viking* on the Bering Sea and that his cohorts, about five in all, were his crew.

Mary found this Phil guy interesting. There was definitely something different about him.

Phil invited Mary outside for some air and a drink. She liked his relaxed, upbeat style. He was brimming with self-esteem, yet didn't come across as arrogant.

They talked for a while, sharing some laughs on one of those rare Washington nights when the stars are actually visible.

Mary opened up to Phil, telling him about her violent husband. Phil said she should let him know that, if he didn't cool it, Phil would have some very serious people pay him a visit.

Phil told Mary he'd be back at eleven when she got off work. As she came strolling out of the bar, there was Phil standing beside his red Corvette. He came running around to the passenger side and opened the door for her.

As they roared away, Mary didn't notice the white powder on a hand mirror resting on the console. She rolled down her window to flick away a few ashes from her cigarette. As she did so, some of that white powder joined the ashes disappearing into the night.

As she turned back, Mary noticed a disgusted look on Phil's face.

"Uh, you rolled the window down," he said.

"Yeah," said Mary, wondering why that was a problem.

"Did you notice all the powder on that mirror that got blown away?" Phil asked.

"Oh, I'm sorry," she said.

"Don't worry," Phil said. "That was only about three hundred dollars' worth of coke."

"Coke?" Mary asked.

"You've never had any?" said Phil.

"No," she insisted, then got right to the point: "And I want you to know that you're not getting laid tonight. If that's what you're expecting, you can drop me back at the club right now."

"You have nothing to worry about," Phil assured her.

They wound up at the *Golden Viking*, where they sat talking until dawn.

Mary was intrigued. Who was this new man in her life and what did he mean to her future?

She soon found out. Phil would call in the early morning hours on a daily basis to see that she'd made it home safely from work and that hubby was keeping his mittens to himself. Phil treated her like a queen, telling her that she was gorgeous and alluring, and that she was destined to one day be his wife.

"But I'm already married," she would say.

Phil would shrug and say, "That's just a small obstacle."

Smaller all the time. Phil had come into Mary's life just as her marriage was crumbling, and her husband was spending less and less time at the house.

Phil asked Mary to lunch a few days after they met and flew her to San Francisco, where they dined at a five-star bistro.

Mary never knew what to expect next, but she knew that, with Phil around, she would never be bored. He called her every two hours. He smothered her in dozens of expensive long-stemmed roses.

Mary's neighbors were perplexed by the sight of flower shop delivery vans day and night. When friends dropped by, they would think, Wow, did somebody die?

Phil himself would often drive by her house several times a night on his Harley-Davidson. Mary's husband and everyone else in the neighborhood would hear him roar through.

Mary's husband finally split after six years of marriage, but he came by one time when Phil was visiting. Mary braced for an eruption. Instead, she was stunned to see her ex cruising off on Phil's Harley. Phil explained to Mary that the ride would keep her estranged husband busy, allowing him and Mary some private time together.

This is nuts, she thought.

By the time Phil met Mary, he was well into his hobby of collecting Corvettes. He had a white one, a black one, and the red one.

Mary's favorite story about Phil and his cars, one that causes her to laugh to this day, occurred when they went shopping together for a new Corvette. Phil liked the convertible model, while Mary was pushing for the hardtop. To prove his point, Phil had her sit in the convertible, then he gazed up at the sky.

"Look how open it is," he said.

If Mary had trained a seagull, she could not have timed it better. Phil had long hated the birds for unexplained reasons, and just then, one returned the feeling by dropping a load of poop dead center on his upturned face.

"You know, you're right," said Phil calmly as he wiped the mess off. "A hardtop would be nice."

Phil's treatment of his cars was a testament to his impulsiveness. The black Corvette had been giving Phil trouble around the time he met Mary, so, unable to deal with the downtime required to repair it, he simply sold it.

Mary was quickly learning that patience was not one of Phil's virtues.

Neither was a strong paternal instinct. At the time Mary and Phil hooked up, her son, Shane, was three and a half and her daughter, Meigon, was two. Mary was looking for stability, not riches. Phil knew nothing about children. He would roll through town in one of his Corvettes with him and Mary comfortably settled in the front bucket seats, while the kids were stuffed in the back. She wasn't comfortable with that.

When they were out on one occasion, Phil offered to take Shane to the bathroom. When the two were done, out they came with Shane's pants and underpants still around his ankles. It hadn't occurred to Phil that a three-and-a-half-year-old might need some help with his clothes.

Mary was also surprised to find that Phil, so sharp and decisive when it came to commanding a crab boat, could be a scatterbrain when money was involved. He once took her out for a lavish dinner, the bill running up to three hundred dollars, but when the check came, he discovered he'd forgotten to bring any funds, so Mary wound up paying.

It wasn't as if he didn't have the money. Just the opposite. Phil was dripping with the stuff thanks to his success in the Bering Sea. If he burned up a vast number of greenbacks, that was no problem. Dutch Harbor was always on Phil's horizon.

In just their second week together, Phil took a meaningful step with Mary by bringing her over to meet his father, Grant, and his step-mother, Paula. Mary remembers Paula showing her the chickens in their backyard and their big red rooster, Henry, who, Mary said with a fond smile, chased her around the property, perhaps because she was wearing bright red. Phil also introduced Mary to his beloved grand-mother, Eleanor.

As their courtship blossomed, he invited Mary to his 1,200-square-foot, three-bedroom home in Bothell with the intention of making it her new address.

First, however, he had to clear the decks. Phil had been living with a woman named Cheryl for the previous two years. No problem. He simply waited for Cheryl to go to work, packed up her stuff, and called her brother to pick it up, informing him that his sister no longer resided at Phil's house.

In the middle of Mary's first visit to Phil's house, Cheryl barged in, tears flowing, and a dramatic confrontation played out. It turned out to be the girlfriend's farewell scene. That day, Mary saw a different Phil, an insensitive Phil, and wondered how he could so easily turn off his feelings for his main squeeze of the previous few years. Mary tucked those concerns into the recesses of her mind, vowing to be prepared should she one day fall victim to a similar scenario. The Phil she was getting to know was utterly charming, but the Phil she had just wit-nessed was equally ruthless.

Against her better judgment, Mary stuck around. She soon learned it was a house like no other she had ever seen. People were constantly coming and going. Women called at all hours of the night. Cases of beer, Crown Royal whiskey, and expensive Stolichnaya vodka littered the place. There were constant food deliveries, nonstop drinking and pot smoking, people going in and out of the bathrooms in shifts.

Exhausted by the pace of the never-ending party, Mary was surprised Phil didn't seem to feel the same way. "I wondered," she said, "when he ever found the time to sleep."

Phil could never even sit still. He would knock back a shot of Stolichnaya and chase it with a shot of Pepto-Bismol. He always had a cigarette dangling from his teeth or gripped between his fingers. At times, he'd have three or four going at once.

Mary had caught a glimpse of it on her first night with Phil, but she was soon confronted with undeniable evidence that Phil's energy came from more than just cigarettes. She overheard him boasting that he'd spent $17,000 on cocaine in just three weeks. Alarmed, she voiced her concerns to Phil about his habit, but he waved her off. The way he saw it, he said, he was young and worked his butt off. He deserved to blow off steam during his time on land. Coke? Hell, it was the seventies, everyone was doing it, or at least all the hip, young partiers who could afford it. Besides, he said, it wasn't like he was selling drugs. He was just a happy consumer.

Although it paled in comparison to his other addictions, Phil also became hooked on coffee after buying Mary an espresso machine. From then on, he gave up his habit of beginning the day with Coke, as in Coca-Cola, opting instead for a cup of java.

"Imagine Phil in his twenties," Mary said. "He already had way too much energy. Now the caffeine was kicking in, too."

After getting a taste of Phil's lifestyle, Mary summed it up in three words: "It was insane."

She was referring to more than just the fact that Phil was a party animal. He was also an owner of animals, both live and stuffed, his crazy menagerie adding to his bizarre home life.

Phil's place looked like a taxidermist's shop with mounted skins everywhere. The stuffed animals creeped Mary out, but not as much as the live ones. He had a huge collection of strange pets: snakes, lizards including iguanas, and piranhas, along with rats to feed the many snakes. He took delight in serving up the rats while they were still tiny, knowing that once they reached full size, they became the only creatures on earth that made him cringe. He had no such problem with his two spiders: not your everyday, garden-variety spiders, but gargantuan tarantulas.

One time years later, when Phil and Mary were married and Josh and Jake were youngsters, Mary had the house fumigated while Phil was at sea. It was only after the structure had been covered up and the process begun that she realized she had forgotten about Harold, Phil's favorite tarantula.

Uh-oh, she thought. Poor Harold; he's probably dead.

It was an understandable mistake.

"It's not like Harold jumped up and down every day," Mary said, "and let you know he was there."

Upon hearing that Harold had been left behind, Josh didn't shed any tears.

"Fuck that thing," he said. "I hated it."

"That's understandable," said Mary. "Phil loved to freak his guests out, so he made Josh pick up Harold, the meaner of the two spiders, and frighten people."

When the house was opened up after the fumigation, Mary looked in Harold's cage and thought she was seeing his lifeless carcass. What she didn't know was that tarantulas shed their skin and she was looking at the result of that process. With a sigh, she fought off a wave of disgust, took the cage, carcass and all, and tossed it in the garage.

But Harold himself was, unfortunately for all but Phil, alive and well. He was hiding under a piece of tree bark in his cage and remained hidden even as Mary moved the cage to the garage.

No one knew that for eight months. Then one day, when Mary's kids wanted a home for a new lizard, she remembered the container she thought was Harold's final resting place. She went out to the garage, found the cage, wrapped her hand around a tissue, and gingerly stuck her arm in to remove Harold's supposed remains.

As she wrapped her fingers around the dark object at the bottom, her heart started beating furiously, followed by a loud scream.

The carcass was moving.

It was Harold, back from the dead. He was all shriveled up but still functioning. He had survived a fumigation and eight months of abandonment.

Even Mary felt sorry for him, so sorry that she got him a treat, a bunch of crickets, and filled up his old cup with water.

"He drank for two hours and the puffball got bigger and bigger," Mary said. "He was fine."

There was no telling what might pop up in Phil's house. One night, Joe Wabey, Phil's first captain, came over and plopped down on the couch.

"N-o-o-o, don't sit there!" yelled Phil.

Suddenly, out from behind a cushion popped a snake.

Mary didn't dislike all of Phil's pets. She was fond of the rabbits, hamsters, and, in particular, his three parrots. Chico was Phil's blue and gold macaw. Turkey was Phil's green Amazon parrot. Boo-Boo was a green-winged macaw who earned his name by crapping at random in lieu of letting the newspapers beneath his perch catch his droppings.

The macaws could be intimidating in their own way. One of them once bit a broomstick in half.

"That thing was bad," said Joe Duvey, one of Phil's friends stretching back to his teen years.

Mary also liked Phil's Doberman, Maxwell, at least on the day when she had to rescue Phil from his dog. He had gone outside to get in his car, but found his path blocked by Maxwell. The dog was growling furiously as if Phil were a burglar trying to escape.

Maxwell would listen to Mary because, while Phil was out to sea much of the time, it was Mary who fed the dog. So Phil was forced to call her to rescue him while several of his buddies stood around, hysterical at the sight of a helpless Phil needing his wife to save him from his own dog.

Mary loved it. It was the only time she felt that she, not Phil, was in control.

Lack of recognition wasn't the only reason Maxwell would get in Phil's face. When he drove around, Maxwell was his regular companion in the passenger seat. Phil loved to stop for burgers, but, if he didn't bring out a cheeseburger for Maxwell, the Doberman wouldn't let him back in the car.

"You'd come over to Phil's house," said Jeff Sheets, another long-time friend, "the door would be wide open, music blaring, and there would be Phil sleeping on the couch and Maxwell on the floor next to him, just silently staring at you. You didn't dare get any closer until Phil woke up."

It didn't take Hugh Gerrard, Phil's next-door neighbor, long to realize Phil was a character like no other. In 1978, on the day after Hugh moved in, he left his house to go to work only to discover an eighteen-wheeler blocking the driveway he shared with Phil.

When he knocked on Phil's door, he was greeted by a sight he still remembers to this day. "Phil was standing there, wearing nothing but jeans and a big smile," Hugh said, "his hair looking like he came from friggin' Mars."

"Hey, I'm your new neighbor," said Hugh, twenty-four at the time, three years older than Phil. "I need to get to work, but I can't get out of the driveway. Could you, or whoever owns that vehicle, move it?"

"Come on in," said Phil with a big smile. "Wanna smoke a joint?"

It was seven thirty in the morning.

"No, I'll pass on the joint," said Hugh. "If you could just ask whoever owns that truck to please move it, I'd appreciate it."

"Okay," said Phil, "and come back after work."

Curious after his brief meeting with his new neighbor, Hugh did return that night. Peeking in a window, he saw two Harley-Davidsons parked in the middle of the *kitchen*, parts strewn on the floor, oil leaking all over the place.

Wow, this guy's great, Hugh thought. Who gets to park a Harley in his kitchen, much less two of them? He even had a motorcycle engine in the bathtub.

When Hugh came inside, Phil proudly showed off his stuffed wolverine and his piranhas, which he kept healthy with a steady flow of goldfish and mice, then pulled out Mona, a live boa constrictor eight to ten feet long. Phil kept it in a spare bedroom and would periodically toss in live rats—and the occasional rabbit as a special treat for Mona. It wasn't such a treat for Mary, though. Some of the rats had eluded Mona, chewed their way through the plasterboard, and were living in the wall.

As Phil and Hugh became acquainted that first night, they heard a car pull up in the driveway.

"That's my wife, Laurie," said Hugh, looking out the window.

"Let's go out so I can meet her," said Phil. Rather than leaving Mona behind, Phil wrapped the boa around his neck.

Laurie, a businesswoman, was wearing a conservative suit. As she got out of the car, Phil, after looking her up and down, said, "What are you, a fucking librarian?"

He then proceeded to uncurl Mona and wrap the boa around Laurie's neck. She reacted with a nervous laugh.

"What are ya gonna do?" said Hugh, recalling the scene. "That was just Phil."

No matter how outrageous he got, Phil never seemed to chase people away.

"Phil Harris was one of the most charismatic people you'll ever meet," said Hugh. "He just had that aura that made you want to hang out with the guy. He was like a rock star even before he was a TV star."

The charisma went only so far with Mary. Any thoughts she had of moving into Phil's home ended on the night of her third visit to the house, when Meigon woke up screaming after Phil drove his Harley in the front door, did a burnout on the dining-room floor, and then roared out the back door.

"I can't have this shit around my daughter," an enraged Mary told Phil. "This is crazy, not to mention the fact that I noticed you have a loaded gun hanging next to your bed. This is no place for my Meigon.

"I'm going home. But before I do, I would appreciate it if you would pay me back the three hundred dollars you borrowed from me for that dinner."

With a look of chagrin, something Mary had never before seen on Phil's face, he said, "I don't have the money right now, but if you go out with me tomorrow, I'll give it to you then."

"That's blackmail," responded Mary. "Just pay me back and we'll call it even."

Though she didn't get the money, Mary took her daughter and left. But, as she quickly learned, when Phil wanted something, he became obsessed. And he wanted Mary back.

It was like he was wooing her all over again, but at an even more desperate level. Again came the roses to her door, this time enough to fill several flower shops. Again came the calls, this time every twenty minutes. She stopped answering the phone.

So Phil decided to confront Mary in person. He would drive by her house day and night.

When she didn't respond, he came to the club. She sent word she was too busy to see him, but he wouldn't leave.

Finally, John, the club manager, came over and told Phil that boyfriends weren't allowed on the premises, so Phil hung around outside. When Mary got off work, there was Phil, begging her to return.

Instead, she handed him the gold nugget and chain he'd given her and told him, "Look, we don't have anything in common. I'm a regular woman with two kids. Maybe I'll meet a nice guy, get married again, have more kids and a nice home.

"I'm not a drinker, drug user, sleazy slut, or anything like most of the girls who work here. I'm not even a good dancer. I'm just trying to get by and move on. You don't want the same things that I do. You're just too wild and all you want to do is party."

"No, that's not true," said Phil, all the fire and passion fading from his face, replaced with a look of sadness. "I've never said this to anyone before, but I love you. I'll do whatever it takes to make you mine."

"What about your coke habit?" she asked.

"I can stop," he said. "I'll change, I promise." With a flash of his swagger, he proclaimed, "I'm worth it."

Phil handed the nugget and chain back to Mary and asked for one more chance.

He got it. Mary filed for divorce, sold her house, and, just a month after they met, agreed to move in with Phil.

He was overjoyed, even though he wasn't going to be there. It was May, start of another crab season. Alaska and the lush fishing grounds awaited him.

Phil would be gone for four and a half months, but, nevertheless, he wanted Mary to live at his place. He'd toss his two roommates out, he told Mary, giving her and Meigon some privacy. Mary's son, Shane, was already gone, having moved in with his biological dad.

"I've got eighty-eight thousand dollars in the bank, and you can have access to it," Phil said. "You can do whatever you want to this house to make it livable for you and your kid. I hope you'll be here when I get back."

"Are you insane?" said Mary. "You don't even know me and you would trust me with all that money? I don't believe you."

"Everyone told him he was crazy, that he had lost his mind," Mary later recalled. "I was a dancer, for goodness' sakes. They all told him that I would steal him blind."

Phil's father, whose opinion he always sought, told him, "I wouldn't advise leaving her with all your money, but it's your money. Do whatever you want."

Phil depended on his instinct. That's what had kept him alive on the Bering Sea. And his instinct was to trust her.

But before opening his account and his heart to Mary, Phil told her there was one stipulation: she had to stop dancing. Phil said it made him too jealous.

Fine, said Mary, but she had her own demands: "No more Harleys in the house, no more shooting guns in or around the property, no more coke parties, no more coke whores hanging around for drugs, no more drunks camping out on the premises overnight."

A deal was struck. The next day, Phil took Mary to his bank and put her name on his account.

After Phil left, Mary assumed things would calm down, but it wasn't long before she heard a motorcycle come roaring up to the house and found a gargantuan figure on her doorstep.

Frightened, she called Phil on his boat and asked him what to do.

"What does this guy look like?" Phil asked.

"He's about seven feet tall," said Mary, "weighs around four hundred pounds, and he's all hairy and stuff."

"Oh, that's just Joey," Phil said. "He's all right."

With Phil back at work on the Bering Sea, Mary went to work on the house. She had plenty of time; Phil's prolonged absence would be the longest stretch they would be apart during their years together.

First priority: the gun. Phil kept a .44 Magnum haphazardly slung over his bedpost. As a fishing vessel captain, Phil was rigid with safety procedures on his boat, but he was not the least bit careful when on land. So out went the Magnum, eventually winding up on Phil's boat.

Mary also moved the tools that Phil had stuffed in kitchen drawers into the garage and had the carpet ripped out, the wood floors redone, and ceramic tile installed. Then she topped the whole project off with a new paint job, both inside and out. The man cave was turning into a home.

Phil may have been at sea, but his thoughts constantly wandered back to the girl he'd left behind. He called Mary so much from his boat that the phone bill averaged $750 a month.

In those days, communication was ship to shore, and thus all the vessels in the fishing fleet could listen in while Phil was burning up the lines back to Mary. His fellow captains teased Phil no end about his new woman, referring to his ship as the Love Boat.

While Mary loved the attention, she wondered if Phil would still be so lovey-dovey after he saw what she had done to his house. What if he throws me out like he did his ex-girlfriend? Mary wondered.

As she drove to the airport to pick him up upon his return, she was nervous.

She had made sure that she was looking hot, just the way Phil had insisted she appear when she picked him up. He wanted to see the guys stare at Mary so he could smugly tell them, "Yup, take a good look, pal, 'cause she's all mine."

On the drive home, Mary's nerves threatened to overwhelm her. All of her angst disappeared when Phil walked into the house and broke into a big smile. He loved what she had done with the place.

Except for what happened to some of the animals from the taxidermist. Mary had taken them outside to dust them off and had left them there. Unfortunately, a neighborhood dog discovered them and left them in tatters. Phil had a burst of anger about that, but overall, he was delighted.

When Phil went on a subsequent fishing trip, Mary continued her makeover, replacing the old fence that surrounded the property with a new one and adding lush landscaping. The change was so drastic that Phil, arriving home by cab, had the driver go right past his house. Phil hadn't recognized it. Again, he enthusiastically approved the changes.

Feeling she had some momentary clout in their relationship, Mary decided to undergo a personal makeover in the form of breast enhancement. Phil tried to talk her out of it, saying she was already beautiful enough and that enlarging her chest would only stir up trouble by attracting additional suitors. Flattered by his comments and touched by his insecurity, Mary nevertheless went through with the surgery.

Once crab season ended, Mary became part of the Phil Harris whirlwind. They would ride the Harley to Mount Rainier. Phil enjoyed taking her on many of the winding mountain roads that cut through the picturesque countryside of the Pacific Northwest. He and Mary would often stop to enjoy picnic lunches and some spontaneous lovemaking. Mary was beginning to think she had found true love at last.

Phil and Mary would go camping, to home shows, car shows, car races, horse races, street fairs, swap meets, garage sales, rock concerts, boxing matches, football games, casinos, movies, pet stores, and zoos. They went to Reno, San Diego, and Hawaii. "If something was going on," Mary said, "Phil made sure we were part of it. He got bored easily, so we always kept busy."

When there was nothing else to do, they loved to hang out in bars. He wouldn't dance with her, never did in all their time together, although he did have rhythm, which he had clearly demonstrated in his days as a drummer.

But Phil kept finding other ways to please Mary. He once took her to Waldo's Tavern, a bar in Kirkland, Washington, just northeast of Seattle, where his friend's band, July, was performing. Phil had them dedicate the Beatles' tune "Getting Better" to Mary.

It could have been an exhilarating night for her, but instead, it turned out to be a humiliating evening when Cheryl, Phil's old girlfriend, showed up with some friends, one of whom dumped a beer on Mary's head and tripped her when she got up, while screaming that Mary was "a whore, a no-good slut." An infuriated Phil chased Cheryl and her gang away, but he couldn't restore the shattered romantic mood.

Mary had once again learned that, in Phil's world, she could just as easily be embarrassed as excited.

On one occasion, he insisted she join him at a peep show, where, for a mere twenty-five cents, customers could cram into a booth similar to those at amusement parks that provide instant photos. But these booths featured tiny screens where sometimes grainy, always trashy old short films would flicker. They were the porn movies of an earlier era, before the Internet, before DVDs, before VHS tapes.

Phil had discovered the place during one of his nocturnal expeditions along some of Seattle's less-traveled streets.

"Come on in with me," he told Mary. "Just for fun. We'll check this thing out."

"No way," said Mary. "I'm not going in there."

"We'll sit in the booth together," said Phil, making it sound like they were going to take a horse and buggy ride.

Reluctantly, Mary agreed. But the minute Phil stuck a quarter in the slot, she regretted her decision as a woman came on the screen wearing only a thong.

"Can you pick something else?" Mary said.

"I'm looking for this donkey thing," said Phil loudly. "The girl and the donkey."

Phil turned the channels, stopping at a woman and a dog.

"Where's the donkey?" said Phil, the volume of his voice still turned up. "I wanna see the donkey."

"Shut up," said Mary, "you're embarrassing me."

The more she protested, the louder he got.

On another occasion, she came back there with Phil and Hugh. This time, Mary was drunk, as were her two companions. When Phil and Hugh finally stumbled out, they left Mary wedged inside a booth asleep. To her great alarm, she was awoken by another drunk, this one a complete stranger, who wanted to get better acquainted. Fortunately, Mary escaped unharmed.

Phil loved to put her in embarrassing situations, like the time in Hawaii when he insisted she join him on a walk through an area known for prostitutes to see if they could find any cross-dressers among them. And anytime Mary objected, Phil had a standard line: "Come on, don't be a prude."

"You couldn't embarrass Phil," said Mary.

Phil had been a wild stallion long before he met Mary, destined, it seemed to those around him, to always roam free.

Mary changed that in one hundred days. After three and a half months of living together, Phil asked her to marry him. And backed it up the next day by buying her an engagement ring.

Had the wild man finally been tamed?

Just temporarily.

CHAPTER 6

STAGGERING TO THE ALTAR

Phil and Mary were like fire and gas.

—*Joe Wabey*

For a while after their engagement, the chemistry worked. Mary kept the house in order and Phil maintained order in the house. The parties were shorter, less chaotic, and more sporadic.

In the old days, when someone would break something and laugh it off, Phil would laugh along with them. Now, he got upset. When it got to be late, he would kick everybody out and, truly shocking Mary, would help clean up the mess left behind.

She wasn't very popular with his friends, who referred to her as Scary Mary or the Warden. They even had a T-shirt made up with the words "The Warden" on the front and howled with delight when Mary opened it one Christmas morning.

When they were alone, she complained to Phil about his failure to stick up for her.

"Who's in your bed?" Mary said. "Who does everything for you?"

Phil didn't argue, but he also didn't resist the influence of his friends. Gradually, the inmates began running the asylum again, the old patterns returning. The drinking became reckless, the drugs more evident, the parties rowdier, the guests weirder. Phil knew his stuff when it came to quality party favors. He was definitely a connoisseur, so the inventory of intoxicants was always in the elite class. Pharmaceutical-quality Peruvian flake cocaine and high-grade strains of cannabis were the way Phil rolled.

The craving to live at a faster pace had been gnawing at Phil for some time. Mary had tried to rein him in, but Phil was a racehorse, born to run.

He tried to hide the worst about his resumption of the party life from Mary, but that proved impossible. Especially since, whenever cocaine was involved, the coke whores were never far from the scene. With Phil's appetite for the powder prodigious and his supply seemingly endless, the stream of chicks looking to get high with him was just as incessant.

Mary would get in his face, but to no avail. Hating to argue, Phil would storm out, hop on his bike, and head for the boys in the bar.

"I don't have time for this right now," he would say, "so love ya later."

Mary may have laid claim to him, but, in a tumultuous relationship that stretched to nearly fourteen years, the question of who was captain of their own home was never resolved. When Phil would become too demanding, Mary would tell him, "You're not on your boat now and I'm not one of your crew."

Still, Phil was clearly the engine that drove the relationship, and drugs and alcohol were the fuel. Returning one night, Mary could hear music blasting from the house while she was still a block away. As she pulled into the driveway, one of the neighbors, standing outside, told her, "Oh, thank goodness you're back. That same song's been playing for four hours."

Playing a favorite song endlessly was not unusual for Phil. His addictive habits carried over to music and movies. At sea, Phil would often rock out as he roared over the waves, playing a song over and over, at maximum volume, for as long as an entire day—all twenty-four hours.

"He was a guy who could kill a song for you, no matter how much you liked it," said Jeff Conroy, a *Deadliest Catch* producer on Phil's boat.

Phil was the same way with videos. When *Top Gun* came out, he set up a top-of-the-line home theater and played the Tom Cruise pilot flick day and night, watching it more than seventy times. He even became hooked on the soap opera *General Hospital*. He would watch every episode when he was home and have them taped when he was gone.

"Phil was like that," said Russ Herriott, his business manager. "If he was having a good time, he just kept at it. If he wasn't having fun, he'd be off trying a hundred different things until he found another source of enjoyment."

Phil could be obsessive, but the same song for four hours in a row in the middle of the night, with the music echoing down the street? Mary knew something was wrong.

Going into the house, she found Michael Jackson's "Billie Jean" on the stereo, the repeat button in the on position, and Phil passed out on the couch.

Phil always seemed to keep the neighbors happy, though, no matter how unruly he became. The keys to his success: his infectious charm and the twenty-five-pound boxes of crab he brought home whenever he returned from the sea.

It was not unusual for Phil, upon returning after fishing for months, to knock on Hugh and Laurie Gerrard's bedroom window at 3:00 a.m., shouting, "Good morning!" while hoisting a box of crab legs for his friends. When Laurie would catch a glimpse through her window of Phil wearing his Jack Nicholson grin, she would say, with a groan, "Oh no, he's back."

Those around Phil were always kidding him about his sense of time and season. He didn't have any. Day or night, early or late, hot weather or cold, Phil never seemed to notice the difference.

He might hop on his motorcycle in the middle of the night in a

T-shirt in the dead of winter and take off. After a few miles, it would suddenly occur to him that he was cold. So he'd head for the home of his nearest friend, Hugh or Jeff Sheets or Joe Duvey.

"I'm cold," he'd say. "Can I borrow a sweatshirt?"

Phil's return from a fishing trip also meant enough chemical enhancements to ensure a high-octane run of days, each filled with enough outrageous behavior to make Phil worthy of a reality show long before *Deadliest Catch* was ever conceived.

Along with the drinking and the drugs, Phil also loved to gamble, and when those elements were mixed, the result could be toxic. His stubborn streak exacerbated the bad chemistry.

He'd have Mary cringing as she watched him burn through mountains of chips during their casino outings. She witnessed Phil torch three hundred dollars every three seconds at many a blackjack table.

Mary recalled pit bosses at a Lake Tahoe resort once urging Phil to keep playing even though he was in an alcoholic stupor. Phil's losses mounted until the night culminated with him falling onto the table and knocking everyone's drinks over.

One of the strangest things about Phil's gambling was that, at the same time, he was not a spendthrift. Phil's friend Dan recalls that Phil would go to thrift shops to buy his jeans. He'd purchase a stack at a time, explaining that he wasn't "gonna pay big money" for pants when he could get them so much cheaper. Then he'd head to a casino and blow five grand at a blackjack table.

Another time, Phil was gambling at Harrah's in Tahoe, accompanied by Hugh. While Phil became deeply engrossed in playing blackjack, Hugh was busy getting hammered on the complimentary drinks that kept coming his way.

One of Phil's favorite bartenders, Neil, was supplying the booze. Seeing Hugh spill drink after drink on the gaming table, Neil, as his shift ended, told Phil, "You should take your buddy home."

Replied Phil, "Fuck that. If he goes, I go."

They stayed. The next night when Neil returned for his shift, Phil and Hugh were still at the same table. Neil couldn't believe it.

This time, it was Hugh's turn to do a belly flop onto the green playing surface, sending drinks, cards, and chips in all directions.

A couple of flops later, the boys were eighty-sixed. But Phil wasn't ready to head home. He had pancakes at IHOP on his mind. Phil loved his pancakes.

When they reached the restaurant by cab, Phil ordered the driver to pull up in front of a huge window, in full view of a group of church-goers who had arrived for breakfast from Sunday morning services.

Phil saw that Hugh was getting greener and greener by the minute, so Phil left him there, half in and half out of the cab, staring vacantly at the good folks shielded from him by the glass.

What happened next was a scene straight out of *The Exorcist*: the window splattered, the customers disgusted, and Phil, seated at a nearby table, amused.

But not distracted for long from his mission. Without so much as a pause, Phil grabbed his fork and dug into the triple-decker stack of flapjacks in front of him.

Finally, reluctantly, Phil was forced to cut his meal short when Hugh tumbled onto the pavement. Phil came out, stuffed Hugh back into the cab, and off they went with the waiter in hopeless pursuit, waving the unpaid bill.

Hugh got his revenge later that day. Sobered up, he was driving Phil's car with Phil asleep in the passenger seat, contentedly snoring after his marathon blackjack session, his bare feet sticking out the window.

When a diesel truck pulled alongside, Hugh, a mischievous look in his eye, gave the trucker the universal closed-fist pumping sign to blow his horn.

The trucker responded with a resounding blast, causing Phil, not eight feet from the horn, to bolt upright, his head nearly crashing through the front window.

Hugh gave the driver a grateful salute, his day complete.

One day, Hugh heard a persistent knock at his front door. It was Phil looking more terrible than usual, awash in blood and in obvious pain, with all sorts of twigs and thorns clinging to his body, the result of careening off the road.

"Man," he said, "I wrecked my bike and walked all the way here."

When Phil pulled his shirt up, Hugh could see his friend had broken his collarbone, the injury so severe that the bone was jutting out grotesquely through the flesh.

"Man, it was gnarly," recalled Hugh years later.

Phil had somehow managed to walk two miles to get to Hugh's house.

"Why didn't you go straight to the hospital?" Hugh asked him.

"Well, they'd know I was drunk and fucked-up," said Phil.

"The hospital doesn't care," Hugh told him.

Hugh gently put Phil in his car and then raced at speeds up to one hundred miles an hour in order to get his buddy to people who could relieve the pain.

When Phil returned home, his shoulder was still bothering him, the joint popping in and out of alignment, but he refused to see a doctor.

"If you don't do something about it," Mary insisted, "you will have problems when you get older."

"I'm not going to live that long anyway," Phil replied.

He proceeded to gobble down a handful of pain pills, jumped on another bike, and roared away, heading for a nearby bar.

Just another day in Phil's self-destructive life.

When Phil pushed the envelope with Mary, which he did quite often, he would frequently make up for it by whisking her away on a vacation at some exotic location.

"Phil knew how to vacation," said Mary. They once spent ten days in Maui, staying in luxurious digs and living it up. But vacations with Phil could quickly change from bliss to torture.

Having grown up in Hawaii, Mary got excited when Phil agreed to let her show him where she'd spent her teen years and gone to high school. "But, as it turned out," Mary said, "he just wanted to sit in the hotel room, watch football, drink alcohol, and snort coke. I was so disappointed. He seemed to have forgotten how to enjoy life without drugs or alcohol.

"There was no in between with him. He was either running around with his hair on fire or he was a total couch potato."

Phil would go fishing for months at a time and return with a pile of money. After he had risked his life, grinding out the grueling hours demanded by the Bering Sea, who could deny him his pleasures? As he reiterated to Mary over and over again, he wasn't hurting anybody—other than maybe himself, he sometimes conceded. So he lived by his unwavering creed: You're only young once. Let's party. And she partied right along with him.

Mary had her own issues with alcohol: she couldn't hold her liquor. "Mary doesn't have a drinking problem," Phil once said. "She's a problem when she drinks."

One spring, Phil invited her to join him in Alaska for a fishing trip. He had convinced her that she wouldn't have to worry about the weather. It was May, not January, and the storms had long since passed.

He got Mary an airline ticket for Anchorage, but there are no guarantees when it comes to Alaskan weather and, on the day of her scheduled departure, fog had rolled into Anchorage, delaying the flight.

Stuck in Seattle's Sea-Tac Airport, Mary went into the bar for a drink. She kept drinking as the delay stretched to sixteen hours. That's a lot of drinks.

"I had to redo my makeup so many times," Mary said, "I thought I was going to have to peel it off with a spatula."

Mary finally got on the plane, but, even after it took off, she was unable to relax. Not only was the flight extremely bumpy, but, as the plane neared Anchorage, she could see that the fog hadn't dissipated.

So, to calm her nerves, she kept drinking.

"By the time we got there," she said, "I was drunker than a skunk."

Gingerly getting off the plane and lurching through the airport, Mary could see, through squinting eyes, the word "Bar" on a sign.

Anxious to get off her feet, she stumbled in, only to find the place was packed with fishermen, every chair taken.

Didn't matter. She could have her choice of seats. From all sides of the room, bar patrons were motioning to her.

"You can sit here right next to me," said one.

"No, sit here," said another.

Or here.

Or there.

These guys are so friendly, she thought, so nice.

Mary plopped down and, empowered by the liquor, began telling jokes, one after another.

You would have thought she was Jay Leno or David Letterman delivering the monologue because all the fishermen at the surrounding tables were paying rapt attention to her.

It was then that she heard someone whispering, "Mary, Mary, get over here."

It was a familiar voice coming from a nearby booth.

She soon realized it was Phil trying to alert her. About what?

In her drunken stupor, Mary wasn't aware she had stumbled into the bar with one of her breasts hanging out.

"That's why I was so popular," she said.

Phil and Mary celebrated one New Year's Eve at a restaurant named Jonah and the Whale in Bellevue, Washington. The booze and drugs flowed freely.

Afterward, they went to a hotel, the Washington Plaza, but became separated after Mary passed out in the hallway.

A hotel employee found her, got her to her room, opened it, and let her lurch in.

Only it wasn't her room. She fell into a bed already occupied by two other hotel guests.

"Who are you?" demanded the woman, her eyes opening to find Mary in her face.

"Who are you?" Mary replied just as adamantly.

Then, the other head popped up, that of the woman's male companion. "Uh oh," said Mary. "I guess I'm the one who doesn't belong."

Meanwhile, livid at her for disappearing, Phil stomped home. Mary made it back to the house by cab, but by then, Phil had already given up on her. She found him in their bed with another woman.

Now it was Mary's turn to be livid. She took off and stayed away for a month, living with friends in Yakima, Washington.

When she finally returned, Mary had a warning for Phil. "Every time you cheat on me," she said, "I'll cheat on you twice."

"Two wrongs don't make a right," Phil told her.

"No," Mary agreed, "but it sure evens the score."

"We hurt each other so much with all that payback stuff," Mary later said. "I would have thought me cheating to get even would have made him stop, or at least kick me out."

Instead, she'd find Phil at restaurants or clubs with women hanging on him or taking advantage of his seemingly never-ending supply of coke.

When Mary would catch him, she would spew her bitterness at his female companion of the moment, then ask Phil in disgust if he was coming home. "He'd stumble back to our house," Mary said, "then pass out on the front porch, where I'd leave him all night."

By the early 1980s, Phil had become convinced that Mary was cheating on him while he was at sea, a belief bolstered by rumors that drifted back to him from home. Jeff got a call from Phil one time at four thirty in the morning. "I want you to come over here right now," Phil said.

"You're back from fishing a little early, aren't you?" he asked Phil when he got to the house.

"Yeah, well, I found out Brad [Mary's ex-husband] was trying to fuck Mary while I was gone even though there was no chance that was going to happen," said Phil. "I wanted you to hear this phone call I'm about to make."

Phil dialed a number, and Jeff heard him describe Brad and tell the person on the line, "I'll give you five hundred bucks if you take this guy's legs out."

Jeff had no doubt Phil was dead serious.

Phil then called Brad and told him, "Hey, I just put out a contract on you, so watch your back."

Brad took off and spent five days at a friend's pig farm, sleeping in a back room while clutching a .22-caliber rifle.

Finally, Phil called back and said, "Okay, don't worry about it. I'm not going to do anything."

He never did, although he wouldn't talk to Brad after that and never forgave him. And though everyone who knew him agrees that Phil would never have followed through on such a threat, it wasn't the first time Phil used the power of a gun to send a message.

Once, when someone ratted out one of his dealers, Phil learned who the snitch was, then lured him over to the house under the pretext of asking for a drug delivery. When the snitch arrived, Phil stuck his .44 Magnum in the man's mouth and told him, "If you ever fuck me or any of my friends again, I'll kill ya."

His temper and his .44 Magnum raised the ire of the local police on more than one occasion.

One blazing hot summer day, Phil, Mary, and Hugh Gerrard were relaxing with a few cold beers when a car streaked by at a hellacious clip, almost hitting Meigon. Phil's street was a dead end, so the reckless driver had to turn around.

Phil decided to greet the offender and point out the error of his driving habits. He planted himself in the middle of the street, sans shirt, like a boxer preparing for battle. But this fighter was armed with more than his fists. He raised his .44 Magnum as the car raced toward him.

It was the ultimate game of chicken, and the other guy blinked first. He pulled over and got chewed out by Phil, but when the lecture was over, the driver took off and called the cops. A few minutes later, they came roaring up to Phil's house, guns drawn.

Phil's friend Dan Mittman remembers the gun being "as big as a hog's leg." After the police saw the weapon, it was Phil who was on the receiving end of a lecture. But, as was often the case with him, he soon won over those who questioned him.

When they asked Phil why he had a gun that size, he smiled and said, "It's the biggest I could find. If I could've found a bigger one, I would have bought it by now."

In 1982, having worn Phil's engagement ring for four turbulent years, Mary decided it was time for him to, in terms he could understand, fish or cut bait. "What am I wearing this ring for?" she demanded. "If we don't stop all this payback stuff and get married the next time you come home from Alaska, I think we should just go our separate ways. You said you wanted to start a family. I'm twenty-eight and I'm ready. I want to do things right. I'm willing to start fresh with a clean slate. But no more cheating and no more craziness."

"That sounds like an ultimatum," Phil said. "I don't like ultimatums."

"That's the deal," she replied. "It's your choice, marriage or cutting our losses before we end up hating each other."

With the issue unresolved, they jetted off for a Las Vegas vacation. Naturally, with his love of all forms of wildlife, Phil took Mary to the Siegfried & Roy show. Mary could tell Phil was really enjoying it.

Then, all of a sudden, right in the middle of the performance, he stood up and declared, "This is the best show ever. Let's leave right now and get married."

"Don't you at least want to see the rest of the show?" Mary asked.

"Nope," replied Phil.

And off they went.

They hailed a cab and stopped to get a little liquid confidence to steady their nerves.

By the time they made it to the altar in one of the many dingy, bare-essentials wedding chapels spread around the city, Phil and Mary were both zombies. And so, in April of 1982, they slurred their "I do's" and were pronounced husband and wife.

The next morning, as Phil walked by their bathroom in the hotel, he saw Mary on the floor, hugging the toilet bowl. Noticing something stuck on her back, Phil peeled it off.

It was their wedding certificate.

CHAPTER 7

RAISING HELL, RAISING KIDS

What woman in her right mind would want to be with a guy who
is never there?

—*Josh*

When Mary got pregnant, Phil got scared.

Bearing the responsibility for keeping crew members alive under the most frightening nautical conditions on earth was manageable. Bearing the responsibility for raising a child seemed, in some ways, unimaginable to Phil. As Mary once said, "Not much scares Phil. Just fatherhood and rats."

When Mary was wheeled into the delivery room, Phil accompanied her, but he didn't stay long. Doctors don't want nervous wrecks hanging over them while they work. Phil was ordered to go out into the hall, where he stood, anxiously clutching his wife's purse, while his first son entered the world.

Eleven months after the wedding, Joshua Grant Harris was born on March 18, 1983.

Although he was premature by three weeks, the baby proved to be healthy and strong. That can be crucial to your well-being when your father has a drinking problem. Although he had hoped for a girl, Phil was thrilled with his new son, but not thrilled enough to give up alcohol.

When Josh was three months old, a drunk Phil picked him up, but accidentally dropped the baby on his head. Fortunately, Josh was okay, but that didn't stop a furious Mary from verbally lambasting Phil.

He responded by pinning her up against a wall before suddenly backing off and dropping his head in shame.

"I'm fucking up," he admitted. "I just feel so much pressure. Sometimes, I just wish I was a bum with nothing to lose."

Mary, worried about her young son's safety, was not satisfied with her husband's response. Neither was a neighbor, who called the police. When they arrived, Phil offered to leave, but Mary saved him the trouble. She packed Josh up, along with Meigon (Shane was with his father at the time), and took off.

She stayed with a friend for three weeks. Phil would drive by her temporary home obviously drunk, shout profanities, and harass Mary.

But no matter how much Phil would bombard Mary with verbal abuse, she couldn't stay away. She loved him, and every time he promised to change and vowed to give up his addictions, she felt that this was the time he meant it. This was the time he would truly reform.

So back she came with Josh after twenty-one days and things returned to normal. But for Phil, normal meant drunk.

For Josh, that almost meant disaster once again when he was eight months old. As he was crawling around the house, he spotted a shot glass full of vodka left on a coffee table. With no one else paying attention, he furiously moved his little arms and legs to propel himself over there and then pulled his small body up.

As Mary's eyes locked on Josh, she saw the last drops of vodka disappearing down his throat. She yelled at Phil that they needed to rush their son to the hospital.

"Wait a minute," said Phil, his palms pumping downward to signal for calmness, his gaze focused on his infant child. Josh's eyes got big, his breathing heavy.

But the crisis quickly passed, and a look of serenity came over his face. He dropped back to the floor and resumed crawling, heading off in search of more mischief.

"He's fine," said Phil, a big grin on his face. "He's just like me."

That wasn't necessarily a good thing. One afternoon late in 1983, the owner of a boat on which Phil was serving as captain showed up unannounced at the dock and found Phil passed out in the wheelhouse from too much booze.

Not only was Phil fired, but, his reputation soiled, he was run aground indefinitely, with no one in the fishing industry willing to hire him.

"We lost everything," Mary said. "Our house, the land, the Corvettes, the Porsche, the Harley, and the parrots. It was terrible."

All that Phil had worked so hard for was gone in the time it took to guzzle a bottle of vodka. As hard as all that was, taking him away from the sea might have been the most painful punishment of all.

Phil and Mary rented a house, he got a job doing construction for a friend, and she provided in-home day care. After all that time he had spent as the boss, with men older than he was taking his orders and placing their lives in his hands, he was now just another guy punching a time clock. It was a humbling time for Phil.

It was about a year before his exile on dry land came to an end. Phil's reliability and excellence as a captain finally overshadowed his personal failings, earning him another boat, *The Dominator*, a trawler operating out of Kodiak Island off the coast of Alaska.

But just a few months later, in early 1985, his main focus turned back to Bothell after Mary again became pregnant. Again, Phil hoped for a girl. He was so certain that he was going to have a daughter this time that he bought a pink outfit for the baby to wear home from the hospital.

Mary felt that Phil's yearning for a girl stemmed from the fact that he had fathered a daughter back in high school. Before the baby was even born, Phil had told the mother he would have nothing to do with the child. He felt he was too young for the obligations that came with parenting. As Mary found out years later, Phil had a tough time shaking those feelings.

Mary went into labor on a stormy night in Bothell. As Phil drove her to the hospital through heavy rain, crackling lightning, and powerful winds, he popped Phil Collins's "In the Air Tonight" into his CD player and turned the volume up full blast.

The first cries Phil heard while waiting outside the delivery room were soft and quiet, reinforcing his belief that the baby was a girl.

Instead, Phil was met by his and Mary's second son, Jacob Charles Harris, born October 21, 1985.

"Well, I guess I'd better take this outfit back to the store," Phil said. "We can't take our son home dressed in pink."

Any disappointment Phil felt melted away when he picked Jake up and held him in his arms. He couldn't help noticing that he had another cute, lovable son.

The money in Kodiak was good, but Phil wasn't happy with either his crew or his boat. He felt that the crew didn't give him the respect he was due and that his boat was a downgrade. *The Dominator* was referred to as a dragger because it caught fish by dragging a net through the water behind it. To Phil, that was a boring operation compared to the challenge of trying to catch crabs by submerging eight-hundred-pound pots in the stormy waters of the Bering Sea.

"This is not me," he told Mary. "I'm a crab fisherman."

Would Phil ever get back to that life? Despite his earlier missteps, Phil was still known from Seattle to Dutch Harbor and beyond as a hard-driving captain who was calm in crises and knowledgeable about the sea and the art of plucking boatloads of crab from its depths. And most important of all, he had a reputation for always keeping the safety of his crew his top priority.

All those attributes soon resulted in offers from owners in the crab boat fleet. Phil became a crab boat captain again, working on several ships before winding up as skipper of the *Shishaldin*, named for the tallest volcano in the Aleutian Islands.

Back on the Bering Sea, Phil was soon living the good life again. And on shore, that meant the high life. He seemed determined to make up for lost party time.

"You know, you're not too tough to die," Mary told him. "Your body is a machine, and look what you're putting into it—junk food, booze, and drugs."

Phil had more than just his own health to worry about. His addictions were also affecting those around him. But Phil didn't realize the consequences until it was too late—until after he found himself to blame for a tragedy that would haunt him for the rest of his life.

Back in the summer of 1980, Phil, Mary, Hugh, and Laurie had wanted to go out one balmy evening but lacked a babysitter for Meigon. Steve Skuttle, Phil's best friend from high school, volunteered to watch her.

In appreciation, Phil handed Steve a bottle of Stoli vodka. Phil had acquired a taste for Stoli after being exposed to it out on the Bering Sea, courtesy of Russian sailors. Phil would trade several pairs of jeans, prized by the Russians, in exchange for a couple of cases of Stoli.

Steve had developed the taste as well, and once Phil and Mary left and Meigon had been put to bed, he proceeded to consume the entire bottle. Upon the return of the two couples, Steve bid them adieu, hopped in his car, and headed for home.

Perhaps he was able to conceal his inebriated state, or perhaps, with Phil and Mary focused on looking in on the sleeping Meigon, nobody noticed. But it would have been hard for anyone in Steve's vicinity on the road not to notice just how drunk he was. He wound up wrapping his car around a tree.

"He basically killed himself," said Hugh.

Not at first. At the hospital, Steve, though badly hurt, was revived. When Phil was notified of the crash, he ran over to the hospital on foot. When he arrived, Phil learned that Steve had suffered massive injuries, the most severe to his liver.

Hugh soon joined Phil in the intensive care unit, where Phil stood helplessly, devastated by the condition of his old high school buddy. When Phil and Hugh left the room, Hugh witnessed something few human beings had ever seen: Phil Harris crying. His tough-guy persona melted away as his anguish took hold.

Along with the grief, Phil was crushed by guilt. He felt responsible for the wreck because he had provided Steve with the liquor that had led to the tragedy.

When it was time for Phil to head back up to Alaska, he asked Hugh to commit to taking care of Steve in his absence. Anything to ease your mind, Hugh replied.

Steve spent months in intensive care, with Hugh a constant visitor. He continued to keep an eye on Steve after he was released, but there wasn't much progress to report. With his liver permanently damaged, Steve was never the same.

Nor was Phil, to some degree. He told Steve more than once that he felt he was to blame for the accident. And every time, Steve assured him that it wasn't the case. But for the next five years, until the day in 1985 when Steve died at age twenty-nine, Phil never stopped apologizing.

"That was the second time I saw Phil cry," said Hugh. "Steve's death really had an impact on him. I think it was the first time a close friend of his had died.

"The ordeal with Steve showed me that Phil was much more than this rough, tough crab fisherman, the character people knew from Alaska. He really had a heart."

The only other time people saw Phil cry was after the death of his grandmother, Grant's mother, Eleanor Van Noy.

"That was another part of Phil's life that most people didn't know about," Hugh said. "Whenever he would come back from Alaska, he would diligently go over to visit his grandmother. He would get her up and make sure she could still move around. He'd crack jokes and make her laugh."

Phil was also there for his fun-loving neighbor and friend, Hugh Gerrard, when Hugh was making a genuine effort to escape the clutches of his addiction. Cocaine had long been Hugh's mistress and alcohol her lady-in-waiting, but in July of 1986, he went into rehab.

"Most of my friends fell off the face of the earth when I became clean and sober," he said, "but Phil stayed true to me. Party or no party, Phil was a loyal friend."

While supportive, Phil couldn't totally stifle his tendency to goad and agitate. He was constantly trying to coax Hugh into taking a shot of booze. But Hugh knew that, if he fell for it, Phil would chew him out for being a weakling and falling off the wagon.

"I was fucked either way," Hugh said, "but I was more fucked if I took that drink."

So he didn't.

Hugh saw other sides of Phil that were never part of his public image. Many times, they would take Phil's small Bayliner boat out to Puget Sound and just hang out, Phil guiding the boat by the stars. He and Hugh would watch television and talk about all sorts of subjects while fishing for salmon.

Their discussions even included spirituality. While he didn't consider himself a member of any particular religion, Phil believed there was a Higher Power in the universe, a force that controlled life on earth. He knew he had been lucky in a lot of ways, and he spoke often about how he believed his deceased mother was looking down on him, watching his back and bringing him good fortune.

Mary wished Phil had turned to that spirituality when he was tempted by his addictions. But he at least had the ability to sense when she had had enough. Inevitably, Phil would reach out, even across the thousands of miles of land and sea, to reel her back in as he had reeled in so many fish in his life.

One time in 1985, right after Jake was born, Phil called Mary and told her to turn on the radio. He had dedicated a song to her, "Behind Closed Doors." And he soon followed that up with another dedication, "When a Man Loves a Woman."

"I could never stay mad at Phil," Mary said. "He'd get angry quickly, yell and say a bunch of stuff he'd later regret. But he never stayed mad at anybody very long. And if you apologized, he'd always forgive you."

Phil was a loving dad, but he was hardly a conventional father. From the time Josh was around four, Phil, after going out with his buddies and returning around 1:00 a.m., would wake his older son up, set the groggy-eyed youngster on the couch, and flip on the TV.

Josh was grouchy, of course, as any four-year-old would be after being awakened from a dead sleep. But Phil would solve that problem by pulling out a large package of candy he had brought home. He would invite Shane and Meigon to join in as well, but at two, Jake was too young to enjoy the kiddie party.

Josh distinctly remembers watching old reruns of *Alfred Hitchcock Presents* with his father until 3:00 or 4:00 a.m., two kids munching on their candy, one four years old, the other a sea captain acting like a four-year-old.

"It would drive my mom up the wall to see that," Josh said. "She would be so mad. 'Don't get the kids all jacked up on candy,' she'd yell. It was a wild time."

And a special time for Josh, because with Phil out at sea so much, every moment he got to spend with his father, even in the middle of the night, was something to treasure.

While Phil often had unusual ways of showing it, he thoroughly loved his two sons. They in turn brought both him and Mary great joy, but Jake, in his early years, was also often a source of concern.

As a newborn, Mary recalled, "He cried so softly that you could barely hear him." And as he grew into a toddler, Jake was silent much of the time. At first, Phil and Mary thought he might just be slow to speak. But when he became three, then four and five, his vocabulary at any given time still consisted of only a word or two. His parents began listening to others who wondered if the problems ran deeper than just shyness, perhaps involving a learning disability or some brain defect.

Ultimately, Phil and Mary found, to their great relief, that Jake was simply a very, quiet soul trying to find his comfort zone in a very loud family.

One early spring evening as a heavy rain fell, Phil and Mary took the boys out to dinner. It may have been a wet, bleak night outside, but in that restaurant, the cloud that had long hung over Jake was about to disappear.

When the waitress asked Jake, then five, what he wanted, Josh, as he always did, ordered for his brother, asking for a tuna sandwich. But as he did, Jake cleared his throat and, as if a dam had burst, a torrent of words came out. "I don't want that," he said forcefully. "I'm tired of that crap! Give me a hamburger."

Three jaws at the table dropped, quickly replaced by three smiles. Finally, the littlest one had joined the family.

Phil loved being a family man, but not enough to totally give up his dark side. He still clung to booze and he didn't hide his drinking problem from his kids.

"We would watch him wake up in the morning," said Josh, "and immediately pound down half a gallon of vodka without taking a breath. I could just hear the gulp . . . gulp . . . gulp."

When Phil did finally catch his breath, he would realize there were two wide-eyed sons watching him.

"Here's a hundred bucks," he'd tell them. "Go get some lunch."

Then Phil's head would plop back down on his pillow, his eyes would slam shut, and he wouldn't be heard from again all day.

"My dad was out of control," said Josh. "He was always partying."

In 1986, Phil and Mary bought a house in the May's Pond area of Bothell, a two-story, 3,400-square-foot structure, and the days and months that followed were, in Mary's words, "the happiest time of my life."

Her son Shane came back to live with them. With Shane, Meigon, Phil, and their boys all under the same roof, Mary's home was complete. Mary took charge, redecorating the house, filling it with new furniture, and brightening up the garden with new plant life.

There were family barbecues spiced up with a Phil Harris specialty, his "Bering Sea butt fucking sauce." There were long football afternoons that always drew large, boisterous crowds to watch the games. And there were parties, of course, but they were tame in comparison to the wild affairs of the earlier years.

The genesis of the new atmosphere in the Harris household was Phil's decision to finally deal with his addictions. Seeing how Hugh had changed after rehab and feeling the responsibility that came with an expanding family, Phil agreed to seek treatment for drugs and alcohol. He checked into a rehab center in Port Angeles, Washington, where he stayed for three months.

"There were no drugs or alcohol around after that," said Mary. "Everything was wonderful. Only close friends came by, but nobody else from the old crowd because there was no drinking, no coke."

How did Phil get his kicks in those days? No longer by causing mayhem, just observing it. There was a hill near the house and, in the wintertime, snow and ice would make it extremely hazardous for motorists. On days when the weather was particularly bad, Phil would position himself at the bottom of the hill to watch the inevitable car wrecks.

His kinder, gentler side came out when he discovered Bottles, a homeless man who lived in a cardboard box behind a local supermarket. Phil was constantly bringing the old man care packages of coffee, soup, hamburgers, and assorted leftovers.

One brutally cold Christmas morning, as the family celebration whipped into high gear, Phil's eyes suddenly went wild.

"On no, Bottles!" he said. "I hope he hasn't frozen to death."

Phil rushed over to Bottles's makeshift shelter with hot food, a sleeping bag fit for arctic conditions, and a bottle of Crown Royal to enable the poor man to better celebrate the holiday.

Phil had made a major turn. The ensuing five years were smooth sailing, but Mary knew better than to expect only calm seas ahead.

Sure enough, one day in 1991 as the family was packing for a trip to Disneyland, minus Phil who was up north fishing, there was a knock at the door. There were two men standing there, asking for Mary. She didn't know them, even when they identified themselves as former crew members on Phil's boat, but she still invited them in.

"What do you want to talk about?" she asked.

"Your husband," replied one of the men. "Just thought you should know what a bastard you're married to."

The other man handed Mary a large manila envelope containing twenty-five letters.

"This should be self-explanatory," said one of the men, "unless that's the kind of marriage you have. In that case, maybe you and I should get together, too."

"I don't fuck the crew," replied Mary before kicking the pair out.

The envelope sat there. She took a deep breath, opened it, started reading the letters, and the tears began to flow.

"I was in shock," she later said. "I was looking at love letters to Phil from the ship's cook, a woman named Susie. I thought we finally had a perfect marriage, but he had been having an affair with this woman, who worked in the galley, for a year. How could I not know this?"

As Mary kept reading, the phone rang. It was Phil. He was in a great mood, calling to say he'd be home in a few days. Not knowing how to react, she hung up. He called back a few times, only to wind up with a click and a dial tone each time.

There was a phone number on one of the letters. Calling it, Mary discovered she was speaking to Susie. Mary invited her over and they talked all night. Before she left, Susie asked if she could leave a note under the wiper blade on Phil's car. That was fine with Mary.

When Phil returned home, Mary wasn't at the airport. When he pulled up to the house in a cab, she could see fire in his eyes.

"What the hell is going on?" he asked. "Why did you keep hanging up on me?"

Mary tossed him the envelope. Phil looked at it but didn't speak.

"Please tell me this isn't happening," Mary said. "Why, Phil? Do you love her?"

"No, I don't," said Phil. "How did you get this?"

"A couple of your crew members, who you apparently fired, decided to make a special trip over here," Mary said, "to personally deliver this and then make a pass at me."

Mary told Phil about his girlfriend's visit to the house.

"She wanted me to let you go so she can have you," Mary said. "Because, according to her, you think I'm such a bitch. Is that what you really think of me?"

"No," insisted Phil, "you're the only woman I've ever loved."

Mary wasn't buying it this time.

"You love how I make you look," she said, "what I do for you, the home I keep. I spend every day and weekends with the kids. I sit by the phone for days waiting for your call. My friends make fun of me and call me the Stepford Wife because I try so hard to be perfect. After thirteen and a half years, I deserve better than this."

Phil asked for one more chance.

"No, you can't have it both ways," Mary said. "Not at my expense. I need you to leave for a while so I can think."

"Oh, come on," said Phil, "you'll get over it. You always do."

Mary grabbed a picture off the wall, threw it at him, and yelled, "Get out!"

Phil stuffed some clothes in a bag and went out to his Corvette, only to discover that Susie had left a nasty letter under the wiper blade and a ten-pound salmon in the back seat. With a parting snarl, Phil jumped into the car and roared off.

He rented an apartment in Juanita Beach, in Kirkland, Washington. Four days later, Mary heard that Phil was seeing his new next-door neighbor, Teresa. And a week later, Phil moved into Teresa's condo.

"Phil had the audacity to bring her to our home when he stopped by to get some of his things," Mary said. "He didn't skip a beat. He just went on with his life as if I had never even mattered."

The split was more than Mary could handle.

"I totally lost it," she said. "I went to bed, curled up into a ball, and watched MTV twenty-four hours a day for weeks. I could barely get up to care for the children. I just couldn't pull myself together no matter how much I wanted to for the kids' sake.

"He called and asked if I was sure I really wanted a divorce. I said, 'You are unbelievable. You're living with a woman. Do I want a divorce? What do you think?' He said, 'Well, I don't want one. Maybe we could try a separation until you get your shit together.' I said, 'Oh, till I get *my* shit together? Fuck you.'"

And then she hung up, on the call and on the marriage.

Phil's tumultuous life with Mary was over.

They divorced in 1991, after nine years of marriage and nearly fourteen years together overall. But Mary figured that, taking away the time Phil was at sea, they were probably physically together for just three years.

Still, as Phil would soon learn, his time with Mary would seem like the good old days compared to what lay ahead.

CHAPTER 8

FROM THE BAYOU TO THE BERING

Every ocean has its own wave characteristics. The *Cornelia Marie* fits well into the wave shape of the Bering Sea.

It treads water very effectively because of the shape of its hull. It doesn't move very fast because it's kind of a blunt instrument, but that's not a top priority when you are crab fishing. First and foremost, because you are idling your engines much of the time, you want a boat that is good at riding over the waves. The *Cornelia Marie* is like a big washtub, giving it a very stable platform on which to operate.

For some guy in Alabama, where the boat was built, to come up with that hull design makes him either a genius or damn lucky. But it works. The *Cornelia Marie* has one of the best hull designs in all of the Bering Sea.

—*Tony Lara, relief captain/engineer on the* Cornelia Marie

Every fan of *Deadliest Catch* has heard of the *Cornelia Marie,* the ship that will forever be identified with Phil Harris.

But what many fans don't know is that there is a real-life Cornelia Marie. Though born in San Francisco, she is as much an Alaskan as any native from Juneau to Barrow. Her family moved to Yakutat, an Alaskan fishing village southeast of Anchorage, when Cornelia was two, and there she stayed until moving to Kodiak Island off the Alaskan coast in 1979.

Although she had been around boats since she could walk, it wasn't until she met and married Ralph Collins on Kodiak that Cornelia became involved in the fishing industry. Ralph owned the 60-foot fishing vessel *Predator* when they first met. As his business flourished, he was able to move up to a larger boat, the 72-foot *Milky Way*. Cornelia didn't know much about catching crabs, but she knew how to balance books. So while Ralph coordinated the crews and led the voyages through the Bering Sea, Cornelia served as his accountant.

In 1989, the couple was ready for the next big step, a 106-foot crab boat. The vessel would be built in Bayou La Batre, Alabama. To an Alaskan, that might seem like a strange place to go for a crab boat, but it was actually a wise choice.

Located on the Gulf of Mexico, the 205-year-old Bayou La Batre is known as the Seafood Capital of Alabama. For decades in the first half of the twentieth century, the town struggled to survive economically, depending largely on the abundance of fish in the area. Local residents used to say, "You can hear anything in Bayou La Batre except money rattling and meat frying."

That changed after World War II, when the town became known for producing high-quality shrimp trawlers. By the late seventies, Bayou La Batre was known as the Detroit of trawlers. In the ensuing decades, all sorts of fishing vessels, cruise ships, yachts, ferries, tugboats, barges, gambling boats, oil supply vessels, and tour boats were designed and built there.

Vessels depart from Bayou la Batre to fish from the Florida Keys to Mexico for not only crab, but also shrimp and oysters. Fish packaged in Bayou La Batre's processing plants is shipped all over the world.

Add to the area's reputation for producing quality boats and its proximity to the fishing industry the fact that labor is much cheaper in that part of the country, and Ralph's choice seemed logical.

One of his friends, an Alabaman named Mike King who owned a ship named *The Rebel*, recommended Bayou La Batre shipbuilder Elmo Horton to do the work.

The first of three crab boats built by Horton, Ralph and Cornelia's vessel was 28 feet wide and weighed in at 289 gross tons. The vessel is powered by twin Mitsubishi engines that put out 630 horsepower, with a gas tank that tops off at 25,800 gallons. Cost to build it: $1.5 million. When it came time to name the ship, it was a no-brainer. Ralph would honor his wife.

Elmo Horton is dead now, and his company gone, but his skill and craftsmanship live on and are celebrated around the world every time the *Cornelia Marie* appears on screen.

Ralph's plan was to sail the new boat from the Gulf of Mexico down the east coast of South America, through the Panama Canal, and up the West Coast all the way to Seattle. But just as the *Cornelia Marie* arrived at the canal in December of 1989, the United States invaded Panama with the goal of deposing dictator Manuel Noriega, and, for the only time in its history, the canal was closed for military reasons.

Although it was reopened for daylight operations the next day, the disruption of shipping traffic caused a major delay in the *Cornelia Marie*'s voyage. Ralph sat anchored in a waiting line in hundred-degree heat for eight days before his turn finally came to get through the canal. By the time he reached Seattle, it was the first of March and the crab season was well under way.

With no time to search for a captain, Ralph himself served in that capacity that first season. But, if he could find the right man, Ralph hoped it would also be his last season as the full-time occupant of the wheelhouse. He didn't want to spend all of his time on dry land, but he already had many poles in the water with various financial interests in the fishing industry. Adding long periods at sea on the *Cornelia Marie* year round was not a consideration. "You've got to have some kind of a life," Ralph said.

He and Cornelia were looking for someone they could trust to run much of the operation on his own. For motivation beyond his salary, they would offer their new captain a piece of the pie, part ownership of the boat.

Who would that captain be? While Ralph ran the *Cornelia Marie* that first year, he found himself often within view of another crab boat, the *Shishaldin*. The two boats fished the same territory and seemed to catch a similar amount of crab. Whenever Ralph went back to port to off-load his catch, there was the *Shishaldin* and its captain, Phil Harris, doing the same.

When Ralph brought the *Cornelia Marie* down to Seattle to put in new motors and do other work at a shipyard, he invited Phil to drive over from Bothell.

Phil showed up with Murray Gamrath, whom he planned to use as his relief skipper/engineer. What sticks out in Cornelia's mind from her first meeting with Phil was his knowledge of boats and his in-your-face confidence.

"I didn't find out until years later that he'd never engineered a boat," said Cornelia.

Phil liked to run his boat on instinct, feel, and the knowledge gathered from the better part of a lifetime at sea. He compensated for his lack of technical expertise by always hiring a competent engineer. It's not like he was lost in an engine room. He had a fundamental understanding of every piece of equipment on board. He was just not interested in the minutiae of operation manuals or blueprints. But he could damn well understand the readings on every gauge and point out any suspicious sound or vibration on the boat before his crew, including sometimes even his engineer, picked up on it.

Phil had an innate confidence that, even if a disaster cost him his key crew members and robbed him of his tools, he could still use his bare hands to fix anything that went wrong. And that confidence eased any concerns his crew might harbor.

"Phil talked very fast," said Cornelia of that first meeting. "He was real nervous and smoked a lot, but then, back in those days, almost everybody in the industry smoked."

Having heard enough from others to know this was the man he was looking for, and having seen nothing that changed his mind when he and Phil came face to face, Ralph moved quickly. He and Phil struck a deal at that very first meeting.

After agreeing to Ralph's conditions, from the profit margin to be generated to the maintenance of the boat, Phil was offered one-quarter ownership in the *Cornelia Marie*. His chance to operate a state-of-the-art ship and his first opportunity to own a piece of the action? Phil was, for perhaps the only time in his life, speechless.

But he did manage to utter one word, the word Ralph was looking for: "Yes."

"He had nothing to lose because he didn't have the money to buy a boat of his own," said Ralph. "On my end, I got a guy who was a good fisherman and took care of the boat. And, having seen others leave for better offers, I figured, if I had a guy with equity in the *Cornelia Marie*, it would be harder for him to walk away.

"He got a quarter interest in the boat the day I met him and he kept it until the day he died."

Ralph continued to skipper the boat on occasion, fishing for halibut, while Phil was in command in the hunt for crab.

With the power of part ownership and a boat beneath his feet worthy of the toughest challenges the Bering Sea could send its way, Phil knew the third element he would need for success was a crew capable of matching his passion, determination, and skill.

He trusted Murray Gamrath to serve as relief skipper/engineer, but he would need another crew member, equally versatile, to take over when either he or Murray wasn't there or was heeding the demand of his body for a few precious hours of sleep.

While out on the Bering Sea, Phil looked out the window of his wheelhouse as if the man he was looking for was going to appear before him. And sure enough, he did.

Fishing near the *Cornelia Marie* was the *Seabrooke*. Phil knew all the crew members on every boat in the fleet, and he knew that Tony Lara was one of the best of the group, a multitalented, hardworking crabber. He also knew, from the scuttlebutt that floats around every bar in Dutch Harbor, that Tony didn't get along with his captain.

So Phil, never known for subtlety, called the *Seabrooke* and asked the captain to put Tony on the phone. Even though Phil and Tony had never met, Phil acted as if they were old buddies, telling him gruffly, "I hear you're getting off the *Seabrooke*. Come work for me."

Tony said he wasn't so sure he was getting off the *Seabrooke*, and he was sure that, if he did, he didn't want to hop right onto another crab boat without a break.

For four days the two ships fished in the same area, and for four days Phil kept calling Tony, insisting that he jump ship and join Phil's crew.

Finally, Tony relented, telling Phil, "Fine, screw it. I'll come to work for you."

Tony never regretted his decision.

"I liked Phil," he said. "We butted heads because I was a prima donna, but I learned a lot from him and respected him."

Some of that high regard was generated by Phil's treatment of his deckhands, who would generally work twenty hours and sleep four.

"If you're not in pain, you're not crab fishing," said Tony. "You can work your crew real hard, but you've got to respect them and take care of them. Phil protected us, driving the boat in a manner that kept us safe. He taught me a lot that helped me when I was a captain. The biggest thing I learned was to hire a good crew, get people who want to be there.

"Phil didn't micromanage the boat. When I ran the boat, he left me alone. When he'd take time off to go home, he'd tell me, 'It's in your hands. I can't run the boat from Seattle.' "

While Phil may appear ferocious to *Deadliest Catch* viewers, that's not the way he was with his crew.

"He wasn't a yeller," said Tony. "He'd insult you if you screwed up, but that didn't happen very often. Because of the standards Phil applied in hiring his deckhands, there weren't any idiots among them. We had a crew that was dedicated to catching crab, so he didn't need to crack the whip to get us to work."

The *Cornelia Marie* was grey and white when Phil became the captain. As was usually the case, he had his own idea. He wanted blue and yellow, and that's what he got, giving the vessel a distinctive look that would one day be recognized around the world.

Five years later, in 1995, Phil had another eyebrow-raising idea. He wanted to expand the boat, cutting into the middle of the hull to add twenty-one feet to the ship's length. That would enable the *Cornelia Marie* to take on more fuel and accommodate more holding tanks, placing it among the world's largest crab boats in terms of capacity for hauling crab.

"He had talked about that a lot, but I was against it at first," Ralph said.

Ralph eventually gave in. The estimated cost to stretch the boat was $200,000. Looking at the promise of long-term profits, he and Cornelia took out a loan to finance the job.

"It was kind of scary to borrow so much and not know for sure if it would pay off," she said, "but Phil convinced us it was the right move, and it was."

Ralph disagrees to this day. "I wish we'd never done it," he said. "We almost had the boat paid for at that point. So we added another two hundred thousand dollars for the work, but then guess what? The crane wasn't big enough. It looked like a toothpick up there."

Cost of a new crane: $40,000.

"Then guess what?" he said. "The engines weren't big enough."

Cost of two new engines: more than $200,000.

There seemed no end to it, said Ralph. Every change led to another change, from tubes to shafts to pumps.

Final cost of the entire project: around $1.5 million.

"It cost us almost as much to stretch the boat," he said, "as it cost to build it in the first place."

And the benefits, according to Ralph, did not materialize as anticipated. Lengthening the vessel increased its capacity from 200,000 pounds of crab to 300,000. But the extra time at sea required to catch the additional load ate up a large chunk of the profits.

The expansion work was done north of Seattle in a Puget Sound shipyard. The hours of retrofitting were long and the work grueling, but baseball provided a welcome respite. Tony, his brother Dean, and some of the shipyard workers regularly attended Seattle Mariner games at the Kingdome during the time the *Cornelia Marie* was being stretched.

The 1995 season ended with the California Angels tied with the Mariners for the final American League postseason spot. There would be a one-game playoff at the Kingdome.

Tony's brother got in line early on the morning playoff tickets went on sale and was able to get enough seats to include Tony and Phil. "We're going to see the Mariners," Tony told his captain.

"Oh no," said Phil. "We can't do that, because today is the day we get fuel for the boat."

He suggested that Tony give the tickets to Teresa, who was by then Phil's wife, and one of her girlfriends.

When the first pitch was thrown, Tony and his fellow workers were waiting on the *Cornelia Marie* for Phil, but he was nowhere to be seen. Not then. Not all day. Nor did they ever learn where he had been.

"We sat there," remembered Tony, "tied to the damn dock, waiting to go get fuel, listening to the game on radio, knowing that Teresa and her little friend were sitting in our seats.

"Phil might have died a lot younger and never been on television if he had shown up at the boat that day," joked Tony.

Despite all the success Phil enjoyed aboard the *Cornelia Marie*, it took until 1996, six years after he took control of the ship, before he felt he had finally gained the respect of the top crab boat captains on the Bering Sea.

That respect came, in Phil's mind, not on the high seas, but on dry land in a meeting room in Dutch Harbor. It came not after a chilling encounter with a giant wave, but after a hot debate among crabbers about the pros and cons of a possible labor strike.

As the group was breaking up, Kevin Campbell, owner of the *Arctic Lady* and one of the leaders of the crab fleet, came up to Phil to get his opinion.

Phil responded matter-of-factly, as if he had those kinds of conversations all the time, but what he kept hidden was a feeling of deep satisfaction. The rowdy, stringy-haired rebel who had long suffered from a lack of credibility was finally being taken seriously, his views sought, his leadership recognized. The man who had covered up his insecurity with bravado needed to do so no longer.

"Phil had been labeled a wild man when he was younger," said Sig Hansen, "a roughneck and a little crazy. That was his reputation and it stuck with him for a long time because that's the way it is with crab fishermen. It's a small-town mentality."

When he came back from the meeting, Phil, a big smile on his face, told Tony, "I finally made it in the industry. Two years ago, Kevin Campbell wouldn't have given me the time of day."

Once given the recognition he had long sought, Phil was impossible to shut up. Keith Colburn, captain of the *Wizard*, remembers Phil at some 1999 meetings of the Alaska Independent Fishermen's Marketing Association, the organization that represents fishermen in negotiations with seafood processors. There were three hundred to four hundred fishermen in the room trying to decide whether to stay on strike or accept the going price for crab.

"You get that many fishermen in a room," Colburn said, "and you can't even agree on what kind of bait to put in a pot, let alone whether we should try to get another dime or fifteen cents or a quarter a pound for crab.

"But one thing we knew for sure. Once we opened it up for questions, we would be treated to one of Phil Harris's very colorful opinions, given to us in that crackly voice."

But nobody knew for sure which way that opinion would swing until Phil opened his mouth.

"One day, he would be the biggest proponent of everybody staying in town," said Colburn, "warning that if anybody tried to head out to sea, he would be shot. Three or four days later, Phil would be telling us why we were making a mistake tying our boats up.

"But he had a good sense of timing about that sort of thing. More times than not, his opinion was correct, because he knew the business. One thing is certain. When he spoke, everybody listened."

On one of Phil's first trips aboard the *Cornelia Marie*, Cornelia Marie herself came along. As co-majority owner, she decided she couldn't really understand the business that had become her life's work if she continued to keep her head buried in an accounting book. So Cornelia decided it was time she inhaled the sea air and felt the roll of the waves.

Phil wasn't about to put her in harm's way by taking her out into the middle of the Bering Sea in the dead of winter. But he did allow her on board for the calmer seas of the salmon summer season.

At least calmer by a fisherman's standards. When the *Cornelia Marie* hit the waves, Cornelia hit the floor, too seasick to get up. She was either there or hanging over the toilet. The crew learned to step over her but never ignored her. After all, she was one of the owners. They brought her water, ginger ale, and whatever else she could consume.

After about a week, with Cornelia's stomach beginning to settle, she assumed her duties. Phil had her working as the ship's cook, but he also put her in the rotation on anchor watch so she had some understanding of the mental and physical stress endured by the crew.

While Cornelia may have struggled in Phil's world, the captain was much more comfortable in Cornelia's workplace. He could sit down in her accounting office and accurately figure out the bottom line when it came to overhead and expenses, including the salaries of his crew, doing the math in his head without so much as looking at a calculator.

But he knew the numbers were Cornelia's department.

"I never had to worry about what was going on with the boat, and Phil never had to worry about the books or how the money was coming in," Cornelia said. "He'd call me and get the answers he needed, and I'd call him and get the answers I needed."

The *Cornelia Marie* fished for crab and halibut, but also for salmon and herring. January was the start of opilio crab season, April for herring tendering, July for salmon, and September for king crab.

"Phil had a good reputation as a captain," said Sig, a close friend but a chief rival in the days when both were leading men on *Deadliest Catch*. "He was really aggressive when it came to going after the crab."

But in the last few years leading up to Tony's departure from the *Cornelia Marie* in 2000, some of Phil's enthusiasm for crab fishing waned.

"He still liked the gravy part of the job," said Tony, "actually catching the crab, but not everything else before and after. The crew and I would get the gear ready, the bait would be loaded on board, we'd be ready to go fishing, and that's when Phil would show up. And he'd fly out before the last crab was off the boat."

Tony was able to shrug and laugh about Phil's last-one-in, first-one-out work habits, but one thing he didn't take lightly was Phil's drinking problem, an issue that grew larger and larger and eventually caused serious damage to their relationship.

"Sometimes, before we left Dutch Harbor," Tony said, "Phil would lock himself in his stateroom with bottles and bottles of vodka and just stay in there for days."

But the idea of manning the wheelhouse was a sobering thought to Phil. As the *Cornelia Marie* pulled away from the dock, he pulled himself away from his booze.

"He never touched a drop at sea," said Tony.

On one occasion in 1998, the Cornelia Marie was tied up at Dutch Harbor for an extended period while a main engine was being rebuilt. Phil left the work crew, went on shore, checked into a hotel, and stayed there to drink by himself.

Tony was concerned—enough to go to the liquor store where Phil was getting his vodka and plead with them not to sell to him any more. In response, Phil, determined to keep the vodka flowing, paid a local kid to pick up the liquor for him at the store.

"It got to the point," said Tony, "where I thought he was going to drink himself to death."

Desperate to find help for his friend, Tony called Phil's wife, Teresa, back in Seattle. She, in turn, called Cornelia, who jumped on Phil about his destructive ways.

That began the erosion of his relationship with Tony, whom he thereafter regarded as a tattletale. It was the beginning of what became a constant battle. Tony wouldn't back down, because his first priority was saving Phil from himself.

In October of 1998, with the *Cornelia Marie* docked at Kodiak Island, Tony hired a deckhand named Freddy Maugatai. The night Freddy flew in, Tony drove to the airport to pick him up, leaving Phil alone on the boat.

Phil had been by himself on the *Cornelia Marie* hundreds of times, but Tony wasn't comfortable leaving him alone this time.

"I just had this strange feeling," said Tony, "that I needed to check on Phil."

By the time Tony got back, he learned that the deckhands on *Beagle*, a boat docked near the *Cornelia Marie*, had pulled a thrashing, ranting Phil from the water. Phil had left his boat, made his way to a nearby liquor store, bought some booze, consumed a large portion of it as he walked, then stumbled back to the dock. As he neared the *Cornelia Marie*, Phil had tried to focus mind and body to navigate the final few steps to the boat but had fallen short, tumbling into the cold, black water.

"He was about done when they got him out," said Tony.

The incident only increased the tension between Phil and Tony, and, a little over a year later, Tony left the *Cornelia Marie*.

"After I got off, Phil starting running the boat again," said Tony. "That probably saved his life, at least for a while, because he stopped drinking in order to do the job."

Around the time Tony left, Ralph and Cornelia, after twenty-five years of marriage, divorced. The couple's holdings were large and diverse, from their house and a thirteen-thousand-acre farm in Montana to two boats, including the *Cornelia Marie*, halibut shares, cars, and an airplane.

Cornelia got her namesake, the *Cornelia Marie*, appraised at $2.2 to $2.3 million, as her share of the settlement.

"I put my future in Phil's hands," she said.

It was a wise choice for as long as it lasted. For the next ten years, Phil kept a firm hand on the wheel, steering the *Cornelia Marie* to fame and fortune.

When Phil's tenure at the helm ended a decade later with his death, Cornelia could take satisfaction from the fact that the fast-talking, nonstop-smoking, nervous captain she and Ralph took a chance on the day they met him had proved to be a reliable, efficient, profit-producing partner for twenty years.

CHAPTER 9

STEPMOMMY DEAREST

She was an evil creature.

—*Josh*

To Phil, she was Teresa, the new love of his life. But to so many others in Phil's inner circle of family and friends—a circle Teresa seemed determined to break up—she was Satan.

It is believed that Phil's longtime next-door neighbor and drinking buddy, Hugh Gerrard, first coined the name, but that is difficult to determine since it was used by so many so often. He was certainly one of the first to have a reason to use it, since he was one of the first casualties of Phil's new relationship.

When Phil and Mary broke up, it also ended their merry foursome with Hugh and his wife, Laurie. Hugh took Phil's side, insisting that, if Mary had swallowed her pride and pardoned Phil for his infidelities, they could have been reunited. Laurie wasn't so forgiving, refusing to be part of a new quartet.

Oh well, Hugh figured. He would just hang out with Phil on his own.

Not so easy.

Teresa constantly clung to Phil, so if Hugh wanted to spend some time with him, it was going to have to be a package deal.

When Teresa began trying to distance Phil from his friends, Hugh was number one on the enemies list. He and Teresa were soon in each other's faces. Hugh labeled her a gold-digger and a phony, expressing outrage that she claimed to be a practicing Jehovah's Witness but drank and swore like a sailor. She preached that Hugh needed to find God and change his ways or he would be damned to hell. How, he asked, could she hold a Bible in one hand and a bottle of Jack Daniel's in the other?

With tempers flaring and insults growing ever more vicious, their mutual animosity heated up to peak level, and Teresa kicked Hugh out of the house she shared with Phil. Phil just stood by and chuckled, telling Hugh as he marched out the door, "I guess this means you're not coming for dinner next Saturday night, huh?"

Phil had fallen under Teresa's spell and, regardless of the friction his relationship with her generated with others around him, he was determined to make it work, everybody else be damned.

Next on the list to go after Hugh was Dan Mittman, another of Phil's Bothell buddies. The incident that precipitated Dan's expulsion occurred while Phil was home recovering from a hernia operation.

When Dan walked into Phil's bedroom to check up on his fellow cycle lover, he also saw Paco, a massive pet parrot, the type of bird depicted on the shoulder of many of the legendary sea captains of centuries past.

When Dan put his hand up in greeting, Paco responded by landing on one of his fingers. Smooth, thought Dan, a smile breaking out on his face.

Having just finished lunch, he figured Paco was attracted to a few crumbs lingering on his hand, because the parrot kept pecking away gently at his fingers and knuckles.

What Dan should have realized was that Paco was trying to position himself for a shot at the box of donuts Dan was holding, a treat for his bedridden friend. When Dan tossed the donuts to Phil, Paco lost it, attacking Dan so ferociously that he nearly bit the side of Dan's finger clean off. Blood started gushing, enough to make him look like the victim in a slasher flick.

"I grabbed the fucking bird and whacked him against the damn wall," said Dan. "By that time, Teresa had come in and was watching the whole thing unfolding. She started screaming that I had killed her bird."

Phil tossed Dan a pillowcase to staunch the bleeding.

It was a crazy scene: Phil in bed, Dan's blood all over the place, and the dead parrot at Teresa's feet as she screamed bloody murder.

As she had with Hugh, Teresa ordered Dan to get the hell out of her house, screaming a string of expletives at the top of her lungs.

As Dan stormed out of the house, Teresa followed, bellowing that she wanted her pillowcase back. Dan just stared at her like she was plumb loco, got in his car, slammed the door, and took off, officially excommunicated.

And how did Phil react? Was he as upset as Teresa over the loss of their winged companion? Not even close. He just lay in bed howling with laughter, nearly busting his stitches.

Phil's pealing laughter was a sound that Josh and Jake would sorely miss after he departed. Josh and Jake were just seven and five respectively when their parents divorced. Phil would call the boys, but he didn't come by to see them for nine months at one point because of the ongoing tension between him and Mary.

Phil bought the condo Teresa was living in, and in 1993, two years after they met, Phil and Teresa, then thirty-five, were married.

The first time Phil left to go fishing after they became husband and wife, he took her along on the *Cornelia Marie*. During the trip, the sewage tank was opened after it became plugged up.

Unaware of the problem, Teresa went into the bathroom, set up her makeup kit, used the shower and then the toilet. But when she flushed it, a full load of waste came flying out, splattering Teresa, the wall, and her makeup.

Furious, she went after Phil, who, in turn, went after Murray Gamrath, the boat's engineer. While Phil put on a good show for Teresa's benefit, cursing Murray for leaving the tank open, it was tough for Phil to keep a straight face and not laugh at the thought of Teresa painstakingly applying her makeup only to have it blasted away in the most disgusting manner imaginable.

Teresa never again sailed on the *Cornelia Marie*.

Josh and Jake came to live with Phil and Teresa after Mary lost a vicious custody battle.

"Teresa was great for the first couple of years," Josh said, "but after that, I don't know, maybe the pressure got to her, but she started beating the shit out of us."

There was no escape for the boys. Phil was in Alaska much of the year and their mother, claiming her visitation rights had been sabotaged by Teresa, didn't see her sons for the next fifteen years.

Mary said Teresa got in her face when they first met, telling Mary, "I know a good thing when I see it. Your loss is my gain. You have no idea who you're dealing with. Why don't you just kill yourself and save us all the trouble?"

Mary said the court allowed her to see her kids if the visits were supervised, but nevertheless, according to Mary, Teresa lied constantly to keep her from Josh and Jake.

"Teresa would call me," Mary said, "saying that the visitation date had been changed, then make it appear that I was a no-show. She would tell the boys, 'I guess your mother just doesn't care about you anymore.' Teresa told Phil that I never even called the boys."

Mary said she did call, but that only resulted in the most painful moments of her separation from her sons.

"Teresa would answer the phone," Mary claimed, "and say the boys weren't there. I would say, 'I can hear them. Please, just let me talk to them.' Instead, she'd lie, yelling at me over the phone, 'What? You want to kill us and burn our house down?' I'd say, 'Teresa, what are you doing?'"

Mary said Teresa would then call the police, telling them Mary was a danger to the family. As a result, a judge issued a restraining order against her, forcing her to stay away from her boys.

"Even murderers get to see their kids," Mary said. "I had never done anything wrong. I couldn't believe Phil was letting this happen."

Asking Mary about Teresa is like asking a crab fisherman about the Bering Sea. There are many tales to be told. In Mary's case, there is no way to verify some of them, since both Phil and Teresa are dead.

Mary alleges that Teresa tricked Phil into marrying her by claiming she was about to receive $5 million in a divorce settlement. Teresa also said she was suffering from terminal cancer and, when she died, she would leave Phil the $5 million. The money, said Mary, never appeared and, after Phil and Teresa exchanged vows, the cancer disappeared.

Mary also claims she heard Teresa had hired a hit man to kill her. Mary didn't take the rumor seriously until a stranger approached her on the street and told her he had indeed been offered money to make her disappear permanently. He said he was promised five thousand dollars up front and five thousand more after eliminating her, but had told Teresa he wasn't interested.

That didn't mean, he said, that someone else wouldn't accept Teresa's offer.

"What am I supposed to do?" asked an alarmed Mary.

"Watch your back," said the stranger before going back into the shadows.

Mary went to the Bothell Police Department but was told there was nothing they could do unless they had more details.

"Well, if I wind up dead," Mary replied, "at least you'll know where to start looking for the killer."

Josh and Jake have their own horror stories about Teresa.

Having endured Phil's long absences at sea, she was desperate for attention when he returned home.

"She wanted all his time," Josh said.

His sons, of course, wanted a share, even if just a small share, of their dad's affection as well.

"She'd get pissed that we were even around," said Josh.

So, before Phil arrived, she'd physically abuse the boys, warning them that they'd get more of the same if they tried to horn in on her reunion with their father.

When he was alone with Phil, Josh tried to tell him about the horrors he and Jake had to endure while the captain was off catching crab.

"She not only beats the fuck out of us," said Josh, "but she gets out of control on drugs and spends all your money."

Phil was sympathetic, but he told Josh, "Don't ruin this for me. I've got a great house and nice cars. I've worked my whole life for this. If I get divorced, she's taking half of it."

Phil had done everything he could to make Teresa happy and his long trips more palatable. He had bought a home on Echo Lake, just east of Bothell, landscaped it, put in a pond, a large swimming pool, and a dock for lake access. He also turned one room into a beauty salon to make it easier for Teresa to do her work as a beautician.

"You've just got to maintain yourself," Phil told Josh.

Teresa had her own story to tell Phil about his boys.

"These kids are out of control," she said. "I have to beat them and it doesn't even faze them."

What did faze them was watching Teresa become a chemically induced monster.

"She turned to drugs," Josh said, "because she was lonely with my dad gone so much, and that only made it worse for Jake and me."

One time, Phil came home to find both his sons with black eyes and scratches on their necks. Teresa demanded that Phil mete out even more punishment because of their alleged misbehavior.

"Finally, Dad got it," Josh said. "Finally, he came to accept the fact this whole situation wasn't right."

Phil took the boys into their bedroom while Teresa sat at the top of the stairs and listened, waiting for her husband to fulfill her desire for even more abuse.

Phil loudly screamed at both boys, but then, behind the closed door, he quietly whispered to them, "Listen, I'm going to whack this bed, and when I do, both of you are going to scream like I'm beating the living hell out of you."

Phil started smashing the wooden bed frame while yelling, "Don't you ever disobey. You hear?"

Listening out in the hallway, Teresa reveled in the sound of the blows and the screams of the boys, though she didn't know they were as phony as the whipping they were supposedly undergoing.

When he was done, Phil came out with a look of satisfaction, telling her, "I took care of that."

The boys peeked out of their room and, as soon as they saw Teresa was gone, started giggling and ran downstairs and out the door to play as if nothing had happed. Because nothing had happened.

The smile on Phil's face was quick to fade after moments like that. He couldn't just run out to play and forget about his problems. He still had to deal with Teresa.

"She drove my dad into depression," Josh said. "That's when he started building birdhouses. It was his way of getting away from her. He'd head out to a little toolshed he had built in the back so he wouldn't get yelled at. He'd hang out there all day and night, working on the birdhouses. That's why they turned out so intricate."

"We're not just talking about a tiny wood house with a hole in it, the kind of thing you think about when someone mentions a birdhouse," said Russ Herriott, Phil's business manager. "His houses had shingles, lawn furniture, even a Jacuzzi."

"Making birdhouses was the last thing in the world I ever thought he would do," said Grant, Phil's father. "He never seemed to be interested in woodworking when he was growing up.

"But he started making a few birdhouses and people wanted to buy them. He was amazed those little houses were in demand. I could see why. Every one was totally unique, different from any of the others."

Phil was inspired by more than just public demand. Every time he thought about going back into the house to face Teresa, he decided he needed an added feature, a fancier roof, a bigger porch, anything to justify staying right where he was.

Or staying out at sea, the place where he had always found solace. And now, it was also the one place where he could still bond with his sons.

From the time he could walk, Josh knew there was wealth to be found below the surface of the water. He knew it as a child because that's where Daddy went to earn the money that provided him and his brother with all their material needs.

And when Josh was just ten, Phil told him that, if he wanted new clothes for school, he was going to have to go fishing himself in order to pay for them.

That summer, Phil took his son on a gillnetter, a boat so named because it employs nets that entangle fish by their gills. In three months, Josh helped catch enough salmon to make six hundred dollars.

More than enough for clothes, plus piles of candy. In Phil's mind, since Josh had worked like an adult, he had also earned the right to act like an adult.

"My dad put a cigarette in my mouth, bought me my first drink, and I saw my first *Playboy* magazine," Josh said.

Like his father and so many others who went on fishing boats when they were young and had tender stomachs, Josh got seasick his first time out.

And he got a bad taste in his mouth that lingered for the better part of two decades. His first morning at sea, he was given eggs. With the boat rocking, he vomited so violently that he couldn't bear to eat eggs again for sixteen years.

Yet he didn't get seasick again, and he soon learned to love the time with his father.

"We'd get fish that were bigger than me," Josh said. "When I would pick them up and try to throw them into the fish hold, they would whack me in the nuts. My father would laugh and laugh. He taught me how to drive the boat and set the anchor."

He also taught Josh about both toughness and determination on one unforgettable night. The two of them were fishing on a small boat in the middle of a storm. Phil, concerned that his son was not getting enough sleep, insisted that Josh take the only bunk on the craft while Phil slept on the floor.

The boat had a small wood-burning stove in the cabin and, that night, a pot of boiling coffee had been left on it.

When the boat was hit by a jarring wave, the stove came crashing down, coffeepot and all.

The hot coffee splashed squarely onto the face of the sleeping Phil, awakening him to extreme pain, with blisters soon forming on the scalded skin.

He may have been in agony, but that didn't stop him from fishing. He didn't even consider heading back to port.

While Josh was enjoying life on the water, Jake, two years younger, was stuck at home. Always diminutive in size, he had to wait until he was eleven to be considered big enough to fish. He quickly proved he was good enough as well.

"Jake did a really great job his first year up there," Josh said.

So good that Phil goaded his older son. "He's doing a better job than you," Phil told him. Josh responded with work rather than words, putting in the hours and the effort required to become a successful fisherman.

But while Josh's life at sea grew brighter with every voyage, his life at home became bleaker every time he returned.

Josh had grown too big for Teresa to punish him physically, so she turned to verbal abuse ever more frequently. It became an endless battle between the two until finally, when Josh reached fifteen, Teresa ordered him out of the house. Phil, all the fight taken out of him by the fear of a financially devastating divorce, wouldn't intercede on Josh's behalf.

"Well, I was out when I was young," said Phil, who had also left home when he was fifteen, "so you're out when you're young. And that's just the way it's going to be."

Josh didn't argue.

"I was fifteen," he said, "and I was just going to have to find my own way."

It was a difficult search. Sometimes, he stayed with Grant, his grandfather. Sometimes, he slept on friends' couches.

Josh still came back to the house to see his father, and one particular visit will forever stand out in his mind. Phil was standing on the roof of his fifth-wheel motor home, parked in the driveway, in order to clean it.

"Like an idiot, he took soap and sprinkled it all over the top," said Josh.

Phil's plan was to blast the soap off with a pressure hose, but when he tried to take a step on the slippery surface, the result was predictably disastrous.

He slid off the roof and onto the concrete driveway twelve feet below, landing face-first.

Running over to his father, Josh was horrified at what he saw. There was blood coming through Phil's hair and streaming down his forehead. One leg was bent awkwardly and his breathing was labored. His sunglasses were cracked in half, still hanging from his ears but drooping down under his chin, the glass shattered.

Still, he was determined to play the role of tough Captain Phil, especially with one of his sons watching. He staggered to his feet, waved Josh off, and, his voice cracking, said, "I'm okay. I'm okay."

Phil then tried to take a few limping steps but conceded, "It really hurts."

"Dad," said Josh, "we need to get you to a hospital."

"No, no, I'm fine," Phil insisted.

Josh, too young to possess a driver's license, went into the house to get Teresa.

"You need to take Dad to the hospital," he told his stepmother, who turned to him in an obvious state of drunkenness.

If Josh was expecting sympathy from Teresa, he should have known better. Coming outside, she spotted Phil in shaky condition, dragging one leg as he stumbled around, and yelled at him, "Quit being a pussy. Walk it off."

When Teresa refused to help her husband, Josh went to a neighbor, who drove Phil to a nearby hospital.

Diagnosis: six broken ribs, a broken leg, a massive cut on his head, and a concussion.

For most people, outside of maybe stuntmen and hockey players, that would mean a long recuperation. Phil behaved himself for a week. Then he took the family to Washington's Lake Chelan, east of Seattle, where he yanked off the cast on his broken leg and went waterskiing.

"You could never stop my dad from doing anything," said Josh.

Teresa was the same way. Those who spent time around her sometimes felt there was no way to stop her from drinking to excess.

Mike Crockett, one of Phil's old friends from Bothell, remembers the time he and his wife, Susan, and Phil and Teresa went to a John Cougar Mellencamp concert in a gorge in eastern Washington. While Mike drove his motor home down the narrow, tree-lined back roads to the gorge, he and his three companions entertained themselves with alcohol and drugs.

Then, glancing in his rearview mirror, Mike sounded the alarm.

"Time to behave yourselves," he yelled to the others in the back. "There's a sheriff's car right behind us."

"Teresa was really freaking out," Mike later recalled.

He slowed to thirty-five miles an hour and drove like the motor home "was on rails, straight and steady."

In the back, however, Teresa had become quite unsteady.

"I don't know what came over her," Mike said, "but she announced that 'we can't have any evidence in here, so I'll drink it all.'"

Frantically, she gulped down all the alcohol she could get her hands on, draining the motor home of all the incriminating booze.

"She understandably proceeded to get really, really wasted," said Mike, "beyond anybody's comprehension."

The sheriff's car followed for about twenty miles, but Mike was smooth enough to avoid suspicion. They made it to the concert and Phil, Mike, and Susan had a great time in the gorge. As for Teresa, she passed out in the motor home and there she stayed for the rest of the evening.

Phil soon found a new refuge from Teresa: Dan Mittman's spread in Duvall, Washington, east of Bothell. He had a beautiful home on seven acres.

"Phil would come up and do a big pile of cocaine, but later, he'd groan that he had to get back to Teresa," Dan said. "Teresa hated me, so I wasn't about to go to his place. She was a master manipulator, very good at what she did. If she didn't want you around, you weren't around."

Phil would apologize for Teresa's behavior, but that wasn't really necessary, since most of Phil's acquaintances didn't care what she did as long as they didn't have to be around to watch.

Josh had to be around Teresa if he wanted to see his father, but that soon became impossible. When Josh would show up, Teresa threatened to call the police if he didn't leave. He would look to his father for support, but all he would get was a finger pointing to the door. Then Phil would dejectedly head out to the backyard and the refuge of his birdhouses. If he had been small enough, he might have crawled into one of them.

Josh tried to stay in high school while working hard enough to support himself, but he couldn't maintain that balancing act long enough to graduate. So he quit school and, like his father before him, became a full-time fisherman.

It's not as much fun following in your dad's footsteps if he's got his back turned to you, so Josh longed to resume his relationship with his father.

He figured he had found a way when he learned Teresa was cheating on Phil. Josh came to see him and broke the news, but Phil refused to believe it. Or didn't want to believe it. So rather than turn on his wife, Phil turned on the messenger. He and Josh didn't speak for three and a half years beginning in 1998.

Like his father and his grandfather, Josh felt the lure of the sea. And that pull was so strong, it washed away some of the anguish he felt over his estrangement from his father. It was an opportunity, he told himself, to prove he didn't need Phil to be a successful fisherman.

"I didn't want to live in my dad's shadow anyway," he insisted.

Josh got his first job at eighteen on a dragger, which catches fish by pulling a trawl net behind it. Not exactly the *Cornelia Marie*, but at least a deck to stand on and a paycheck to live on.

He did well enough to attract another job offer. Josh was hired by a floating cannery to work the slime line. If that doesn't sound glamorous, it's because it wasn't. His job was to gut and fillet pollock being off-loaded from boats. It was the equivalent of working on an auto assembly line, except the parts at an auto plant don't smell and they don't stick to every part of the body.

Nobody was going to get a reality show out of the slime line. It was not only disgusting, but exhausting work. With the cannery processing 120 tons of fish every eight to twelve hours, Josh was on duty sixteen hours a day.

And that didn't count his moonlighting job. Anxious for a way out of the slime business, Josh learned that the ship's engineer made a lot more money than he did. So Josh had dragged his tired, smelly body over to the engineer and asked for a few additional hours as his assistant, doing whatever was needed.

What the engineer needed was someone to keep the generator well oiled. Josh was glad to have the work and, when the engineer left after learning he had cancer, Josh became the oiler for all the machinery on board.

Dealing with oil, or dealing with slime for less money? It seemed like a no-brainer. But it was a decision that almost proved to be deadly, an assignment more fraught with peril than anything he would subsequently face on the *Cornelia Marie.*

It began innocently enough. While the processing boat was leisurely making its way back to port, Josh went down to the engine room for his routine check of the equipment.

He was immediately hit with the usual blast of heat, in a room where the temperature could soar to 120 degrees. Upstairs, Josh had been wearing overalls with a T-shirt underneath. He pulled off the overalls, wrapped them around his waist, and, cooler in his T-shirt, began his inspection. When he reached a generator, he bent down to check a gauge.

"The generator was going full tilt," he said, "and the turbo was screaming, sucking in a huge stream of air.

"It sucked the T-shirt right off my back and into the intake and took me with it, right off my feet."

Josh's shoulder banged up against the generator, and there he stayed as if he were a sliver of metal and the generator were a giant magnet.

"I was hanging in midair by my shoulder," he said, "and I couldn't break free. I grabbed a nearby pipe and pulled, but I wasn't going anywhere. The suction was like nothing I've ever experienced. It felt like my skin was going to burst and all my guts were going to get sucked out through my shoulder."

As concerned as he was for himself, Josh was also able to focus on the generator, even in that moment of extreme peril. Here he was, just a kid trying to survive on a meager salary, and he might be destroying a piece of machinery worth seven figures.

The generator began to sputter.

"Exhaust was coming out of places where it wasn't supposed to be coming out of," he said.

Fortunately for Josh, that black, smoky exhaust came spilling out of the engine room onto the deck, alerting the crew.

When they discovered the helpless teenager in the grip of the powerful machine, it took two deckhands, grunting and groaning, to pull him free. Josh's T-shirt didn't make it, the generator instantly reducing it to burned threads.

Though he couldn't move his arm, Josh was still more concerned about the generator's condition than his own.

"Screw the motor," said a deckhand.

When the boat reached port, Josh was taken to the ER, where a doctor told him, "If you had been on there eight to twelve seconds longer, your guts would have been sucked out."

"Half of me would have wound up inside that engine," said Josh. "They said it had happened before and that I was very lucky to survive."

Marie, his girlfriend at the time, did not want him to test his luck any further. She begged him to come back to dry land and find a safer job.

Josh tried sandblasting buildings. Quickly bored with that, he moved on to painting water towers but didn't like working at such heights and he certainly didn't like the sporadic nature of the job. Painters don't work in the rain, a severe limitation in a city like Seattle.

"There was just no excitement for me in any of those jobs," he said. "It just wasn't crazy enough for me."

Josh's search for a new career ended abruptly when his phone rang in 2001. It was the call he had hoped for. On the other end of the line was his father telling Josh he was short one deckhand on the *Cornelia Marie*.

"If you want to prove you're a man," Phil told Josh, "you'll come up and go fishing with me. This is your opportunity to shine. It's red crab, so it's pretty easy. If you do good, you can continue to work on my boat. I know you can work hard, but I really don't expect you to make it. Still, I'm willing to give you a shot."

Phil figured that was the best way to challenge his son, and Josh, anxious to show he was a true Harris, responded.

He started as had his father, as a greenhorn. Phil knew that, if he showed his son favoritism, he would lose the respect of the rest of his crew, but that didn't stop Phil from worrying about Josh.

His concern was heightened because that first trip was undertaken under conditions that would frighten the most hardened of veteran seamen. The winds roared up to one hundred miles an hour and the waves rose to nearly fifty feet.

Josh's job was to crawl into the pots after they had been pulled from the water and the crabs dumped out, yank out any lingering bait, hook up new bait, take a quick glance around to look for any crab that might have been missed, and then get out of there as if his life depended on it, because it just might.

At that point the pots were not tied down. If a big wave hit the deck at that crucial moment, the pot could be swept overboard with Josh in it. Or it could go rattling across the deck, colliding with any person or object in its path, leaving anyone unfortunate enough to be trapped inside severely bruised. All Phil could do from the wheelhouse was to maneuver the boat so that, if the pot got swamped by a wave, it would at least stay on deck.

In those first few days on the job under those conditions, Josh made a decision. After this trip, I am out of here, he thought. This is insanity and I want no part of it ever again.

The thoughts were similar to those expressed by Phil so many years earlier on the *American Eagle* at the start of his shot at crab fishing. And much like his father, Josh reconsidered after surviving and being handed a large wad of cash for working less than three full days.

In the years Josh was out of his life, Phil still had to handle Jake, and that became increasingly difficult as his son grew older. The kid who didn't speak much until turning five was, by the time he had become a teenager, looking for his own distinct voice. That wasn't easy because he was always in competition with his older, more articulate, more aggressive brother, leaving little wiggle room for Jake to verbalize his feelings.

There were other ways to get attention, but they always seemed to backfire on Jake.

When he was sixteen, he took off without permission on Phil's favorite Harley. For a couple of hours he ran the hell out of it, king of the road with the wind whipping across his face.

It was a euphoric journey until he tried to return the bike to the sanctuary of Phil's garage. Pulling into the driveway, he lost his balance and crashed his father's pride and joy on its side, damaging the handlebars.

Jake struggled to get the mammoth machine upright, but he just wasn't big enough or strong enough. Frantically, he called a friend and, between the two of them, they got the motorcycle up and slid it into the garage. Now they just had to pray that Phil didn't notice those not-quite-right handlebars.

Not a chance. That was Phil's baby, and the next time he hopped on the seat, it took him about ten seconds to see what had happened and about five more seconds to figure out who the culprit was.

"I had to replace a lot of stuff on that bike," Jake said, "and that shit's expensive."

After that, Jake was forbidden to drive any of Phil's toys until eventually Phil relented and let his son use his fancy Chevy Silverado. Jake was cruising around Seattle in the truck when he decided to roll into a drive-through Starbucks. Determined to be extra careful with Phil's vehicle, Jake pulled up a little farther out than normal from the take-out window.

The pert redhead on duty, noticing how Jake was keeping his distance, couldn't resist teasing him.

"Is that truck too big for you?" she asked.

That was the wrong thing to say to Cool Hand Jake, who promptly replied, "Well, hell no," slapped the gear into reverse and punched it.

The truck smacked into the railing, scratching up its bright, distinctive paint job.

Once again, the first question in Jake's mind was: Can I hide this from the old man?

He shuddered at the probable answer.

The next day, Phil and Jake were driving another vehicle on a stretch of road in a heavily forested area outside Seattle. The sun was peeking out for one of its rare appearances, and Phil was doing what he loved most, telling a funny story.

Jake wasn't reacting, sitting there silent as a mime, wondering how he was going to break the news of his latest accident.

"Why so depressed?" Phil asked. "You look like someone who crashed their father's truck."

Damn, got me again, thought Jake, giving his father that all-too-familiar hand-in-the-cookie-jar grin.

"I'll get it fixed," said Jake softly.

Phil almost literally hit the roof of the car. He had just been teasing his son, totally unaware of what Jake had done.

"You what?" Phil yelled. "You idiot!"

He eventually decided to just give the truck to Jake, who added a whole new paint job featuring gnarly skulls and flames. Jake still has that Silverado today, a treasured tie to his dad.

Jake may have driven his father into a rage at times, but he also made his dad proud by graduating from high school, and grateful for the crucial role he played in the house as a buffer between Phil and Teresa.

When Jake moved out, Phil was left alone with Teresa. All the birdhouses in the world wouldn't be enough to make that situation work.

In 2003, ten years after they married, Phil divorced Teresa.

While nearly everybody else thinks that was the best thing for Phil, Cornelia Marie isn't so sure.

"I really, seriously believe Phil loved Teresa," said Cornelia. "I think they were alike. They had the same type of personality. Phil put a lot of effort into the relationship. He tried to make her happy any way he could. This is a man who would send his wife a dozen roses on their anniversary every year. He also did that every year for her birthday. He was always trying to please that woman, going the extra mile to try and make their marriage work. His passion for her really caught me off guard. To give that much effort, he must have truly loved her.

"The divorce was very hard on him. I believe it took two years off his life."

Teresa's life ended in 2011 when she died of a heart attack at the age of fifty-three, the same age Phil had been when he passed away a year earlier.

"I didn't even feel bad when Teresa died," Josh said. "She was a mean-hearted lady, one of the meanest people I ever met."

CHAPTER 10

DEADLIEST VOYAGES

Crab fishing is not a job, it's a mentality. You can get past the physical pain. What we endure, you could train a monkey to do. It's when you deal with your own demons, dwelling on them because you have all that time to think at sea, that's when you crack up.

When I get panic attacks, and I've had my share, I try to think about home. But if I focus too much on stuff back on land, I might make a mistake and kill somebody. Or kill myself.

It can be really fucked-up out there. So why do I keep getting back on that boat? Because it's the only thing I know how to do. You get addicted to the lifestyle. You earn fast money and then you come home, party your ass off, forget what you had to do to earn the money, then go back and do it all over again because you ran out of cash. You've got bills to pay and there's no other way you can make money like that except perhaps dealing drugs.

For every full pot of crab we pull up, there are fifteen blank ones. On the show, fans see us bring in all that crab, but they don't see how long it really takes to get it. People think we are out there for a couple of weeks. No, it's more like nine months.

You work thirty-six hours and get four off. It's not real good for your health, screws with your emotions, and you become coldhearted and arrogant. There's no pain in the world like the pain you feel up there in the Bering Sea.

You never know what's coming. You can go from calm conditions with a little overcast to, thirty-five minutes later, ninety-mile-an-hour winds and thirty-five-foot swells. You get slapped in the face by Mother Nature, your face freezes, and layers of your skin just start falling off.

People meet me and say I look a lot bigger on TV. It's not my size they see on the screen. It's the size of my job.

—*Josh*

In 1983, Phil was scheduled to leave on the *Golden Viking* in search of blue crab. While the boat was being loaded at the dock, Mary, on hand for her husband's departure, experienced a weird vision unlike anything she had ever seen. The *Golden Viking* suddenly appeared to her as a black silhouette, no longer three-dimensional.

"It looked like a death ship," Mary later recalled, still shuddering at the image.

She told Phil of her vision and begged him not to go.

"Why don't you just say you want to spend another night with me," he said, "instead of lying about it."

He was grinning, but his wife had ignited an old fear. Phil was a product of a fishing culture that had adhered to superstitions for centuries. Considering the ever-present threats fishermen face, it's not surprising that their desperate desire for a safe voyage causes them to latch on to anything that can give them hope, false though it might be. Historically, some sailors didn't believe in leaving port on the first Monday in April because that was thought to be the day Cain slew Abel. Friday departures were also verboten, as was the presence of bananas, priests, or flowers on board. Some seamen thought it was bad luck to encounter a redhead while heading for the boat or to allow their left foot to touch the deck first when they board the vessel.

After Mary spooked him, superstition kicked in, and Phil agreed to stay ashore.

The *Golden Viking* shoved off without him. And on the first day of September 1983, as it was fishing off the coast of St. Matthew Island in the middle of the Bering Sea, 220 miles west of the Alaskan shoreline, the *Golden Viking* capsized and sank nine miles south of the island. Rescuers aboard the fishing vessel *Tiffany* found four of the six crew members alive on a raft, suffering from hypothermia.

The missing two crew members, Michael McKee and Nick Moe, had drowned. Both were close to Phil. It was a tragic blow, and a tough reminder to the entire crab fleet of the treacherous aspect of their trade. Yet it wasn't something the crabbers could allow themselves to dwell on. Not while fishing in the same waters. Not while there was still crab to be caught. As Phil later told his sons, "You can't take it personally or it will drive you insane."

Yet as Jake found himself asking after his first encounter with disaster at sea, how can you not take it personally when you see the bodies of dead fishermen floating right past you?

It was 2005, and Jake, just nineteen at the time, was on board the *Cornelia Marie* for his first opilio season. The grind of the arduous work was slowly searing into his worn muscles, but he was determined to shake off the pain and fatigue and, like his brother, show his dad he was worthy of the Harris name.

If hard labor and freezing temperatures were his biggest problems, Jake figured, there was nothing he couldn't handle at sea. The ever-present danger and frightening nexus between life and death on a crab boat had not yet been impressed upon his mind. They soon would be.

January 15 dawned as just another endless day of crab fishing. The seabirds shrieked and the waves pounded incessantly at the boat, roaring with rage. But the howling wind sounded uncannily eerie to Jake on that day. A hot spasm ran through his body, surely a harbinger of trouble. He wiped the sudden burst of sweat from his brow before it froze into place, and returned to his task.

Just a few short hours later, the call came. The crab boat *Big Val-*

ley was in distress. Phil punched the *Cornelia Marie*'s motors into full power and raced to the scene, his stomach churning as he rode over wave after wave, agonizing speed bumps impeding his dash to the disaster.

The sight that awaited the *Cornelia Marie* sent a chill down Jake's spine.

"To me," he recalled, "the *Big Valley* was the biggest boat I'd ever seen, so when I heard she might have gone down, I was almost in shock. Then we got there and I looked at the bodies in the water and I thought, Damn, dude, this is real shit going down out there."

The *Big Valley* was a ninety-two-foot steel-hulled crab boat that sank in the Bering Sea while fishing for snow crab seventy miles west of St. Paul Island. Five of the six crew members—Captain Gary Edwards and deckhands Danny Vermeersch, Josias Luna, Carlos Rivera, and Aaron Marrs—perished. The sole survivor was thirty-year-old Cache Seel.

The *Cornelia Marie* was one of several Good Samaritan boats that responded to an alert by the U.S. Coast Guard, supplementing federal and state rescue boats, planes, and helicopters. There had been no opportunity for the *Big Valley* to send out a Mayday call, but its emergency location beacon was activated as it went down.

Seel, who was found alone on a raft by rescuers, was asleep when the crisis began. He awoke to find that, to his horror, the boat had turned on its side while he slept.

"I was dang near standing up in my bunk when I woke up," he told the *Seattle Post-Intelligencer*.

With rescuers on the scene and faced with the anguish of seeing the corpses of friends who had fallen victim to the Bering, Phil understood that, since he couldn't do anything for the crew of the *Big Valley*, he needed to think about his own crew. What they required at that moment was the reassuring feeling of a routine day at sea.

"All right," he yelled, "let's get back to fuckin' work."

At first, Jake just went through the motions, numb as the deaths preyed on his psyche. Finally, he shrugged it off.

"You go back to fishing," he said, "but you're real damn careful, 'cause you know that shit can happen. I never really felt that way until I saw those dead fishermen."

Four years earlier, Josh had seen his first fatality at sea, also on his first trip as a *Cornelia Marie* crew member. It was not as catastrophic as the loss of the *Big Valley*, but it was still a shocking tragedy. A deckhand aboard the *Exito*, thirty-six-year-old Scott Powell, lost his life when he was swept off the boat after it was hit by a forty-five-foot wave while engaged in crab fishing. The power of the onrushing water swung around a thousand-pound pot that was hanging on a crane and sent it barreling into Powell's head, perhaps killing him even before he went over the side. Another deckhand received severe lacerations on his skull, and a third man suffered fractures to both arms when he was caught between colliding pots.

The force of the water not only knocked the entire wheelhouse back six inches but pulled the captain's chair, bolted to the floor, out the back of the wheelhouse and sent the captain flying all the way to the stern of the boat, where he was able to grasp a railing to prevent being hurled overboard himself.

"That wave was so bad," Josh remembered, "that it blew out all the windows, windows that could withstand a bullet fired from point-blank range."

In Jake's initial experience with death on the water, all the damage had been done by the time his boat arrived. But in Josh's case, he was forced to see the terror unfold.

"That boat was right next to us," he said. "We watched it all go down, but we couldn't do a damn thing about it. We couldn't turn around to help them because of the possibility that we would roll our own boat over."

While the jaw-dropping fact that people could and did die all the time in their chosen profession was impressed upon both Josh and Jake by these unforgettable examples, their father had a long and ever-expanding log of such frightening memories accumulated over his years on the Bering Sea.

One of the most painful, Phil told his sons, was the loss of Mike Bosco, who died along with two others when the sixty-five-foot *Bering Scout* crab boat sank in 1981.

After losing his wife and infant child in a car accident, Mike had fallen into a depression so deep that it landed him on skid row.

He had, however, been plucked from there by a sympathetic boat owner who gave him a job as a deckhand. Mike worked for three years alongside Phil, found a new woman, got engaged, and asked Phil to be the best man at his wedding.

First, however, Mike decided to go on one short blue crab outing.

The fact that his dreams of finally finding marital happiness again ended before they began was tough enough for Phil. But what made it even worse for him was arriving on the scene, seeing the *Bering Scout* upside-down in the water, and knowing Mike was under there, perhaps still clinging to life, but also knowing there was no way to get to him. Phil carried that bitter memory with him until the day he died.

There was also the radio cry that Phil would never forget. Actually, it's a cry that will never leave the minds of many captains, because the voice of impending doom went out to the entire fleet.

It came from the wheelhouse of a sinking boat. The vessel was on its side, and the only way out was through an empty window frame where the glass had been blown out. All of the crew members made it through that escape route except for the engineer, who was too big to squeeze through.

Unable to wedge himself out and seeing the boat slip lower and lower into the sea with water pouring in from everywhere, he screamed, "I've got a family. I've got kids. I'm going to die!"

Unfortunately, those were his last words.

A deckhand on Phil's boat was once swept overboard and never found. It was more than five minutes before anyone knew he was gone and, by then, all anyone could see was an empty sea in all directions.

Although Phil frequently looked out the wheelhouse window to make sure he knew where everyone was, and despite the fact the crewman had failed to heed Phil's warning to never go out on deck alone, the captain was still left with the feeling that perhaps there was something more he could have done to save him.

"That's a brutal feeling to live with because you think it's your fault," said Phil in the book *Deadliest Catch: Desperate Hours*. "I didn't do anything wrong, but you can't convince yourself of that at the time. All you know is that they are dead."

It was a terrible burden to bear, but one Phil was eventually able to push out of his mind by reminding himself that, unfortunately, death was an inevitable part of his chosen profession.

"If I didn't accept that," he told Josh and Jake, "I couldn't do this job."

But not all of Phil's harrowing stories had unhappy endings. There was, of course, the dramatic survival story involving his father, Grant, aboard the *Golden Viking* after it was hit by a massive wave, and Phil himself experienced a similar incident on the *Cornelia Marie*.

Having been in the wheelhouse for more than two days on a king crab trip, he was about to turn command over to his relief skipper, Tony Lara.

"It's rough out there," Phil was telling Tony. "You've got to watch out for waves like this one right here."

The wave he had pointed to was big and it was close, getting closer by the second.

And then it was on them, popping open the wheelhouse window, allowing hundreds of gallons of water to pour in.

"That wave," recalled Tony, "also knocked the lights off the top of the wheelhouse and dented the front."

But like his father before him, Phil boarded up the open frame with plywood and made it back to port safely.

That wasn't even Phil's scariest moment at sea. That designation has to go to the time the *Cornelia Marie* was confronted by a wave Phil and others estimated to be one hundred feet high. He certainly didn't want that liquid leviathan to hit the boat sideways, and so, with no escape route available, Phil took the wave head-on, going higher and higher up the wall of water like a car chugging up a steep mountain road to the peak.

Except in this case, there was no road leading down the other side. As with any wave, there was no backside.

For an instant, the *Cornelia Marie* remained poised at the summit of the wave, a crab boat suddenly feeling very tiny at the top of the world. Looking through his wheelhouse window, Phil realized that the *Cornelia Marie* was at the edge of a cliff.

Over the boat went, dropping one hundred feet down before loudly smacking the surface of the sea. It hit with such force that it broke off one of the boat's two solid-steel rudders. That landing set off every alarm on the boat, but Phil was able to maintain control.

When he recounted the story to his sons, Phil laughed as he remembered a call from another boat in the area asking him how the waves were.

"To know, I would have to turn around and look behind me," Phil told the caller. "But I'm not going to do that because I just might have a heart attack."

Almost every crab boat captain has tales of frightening voyages to tell. Forty-six-year-old Sig Hansen, a captain for the past twenty-four years, was twenty-nine when he took the *Northwestern* into a violent Bering storm in frigid temperatures, a combination that generated an alarming amount of ice.

"Most of the other captains didn't fish through that storm, choosing instead to go back in," Sig said, "but I was pretty greedy and still young enough to feel like I had to prove myself. So we kept fishing, but as we did, we became riddled with ice."

Even the spray off the water froze when it hit the surface of the boat. The windows in the wheelhouse iced up, severely limiting Sig's vision.

The wise thing to do at that point would have been to order all hands on deck to concentrate on removing the white menace that was piling up all over the ship.

"I didn't want to stop for three or four hours to bust the ice," Sig admitted. "But collecting so much, you're building weight. I didn't realize how much ice we had accumulated."

The worst spot was the bow, where the ice was four feet higher than the rest of the ship.

"It created a giant soup-bowl effect," said Sig.

The accumulation of a massive amount of water in that bowl, where it would be trapped by the high sides, would leave everybody on board in the soup. And that's exactly what happened.

"When this one wave rolled over the bow," Sig said, "the damn ship started sinking on her nose, then on her starboard side halfway down. I couldn't believe the boat had become that heavy. I learned my lesson."

That offered no solace to the deckhands.

"Panic started spreading," Sig said. "Everybody was freaking out."

He could certainly understand that reaction when he looked out his wheelhouse window. He could clearly see the rolling waves but not a great deal of his own boat, because it was underwater.

Crab boat captains know that the difference between death and survival is often a matter of seconds and always a matter of steering the right course.

Sig calmed everybody down with his quick response.

"I throttled as much as I could," he said, "to get the boat to spin around, trying to get the water out of that bowl.

"Fortunately, another wave came along and hit us on the starboard side, getting some of the water out. That made the boat light enough to come back [level], buoyant, but just barely. That second wave saved us."

Then came the hard work Sig had tried to avoid.

"It took us eighteen hours to get the ice off," he said. "Then we turned around and went right back at it, fishing for crab," undeterred by the near disaster.

Sig's motivation to fish through the horrible conditions was a reflection of derby days, the old system for Bering Sea crab fishing.

Derby days was a lot like another Alaskan dash for cash, the gold rush days. In the 1890s, prospectors flooded into the territory in search of wealth, limited only by their energy level, toughness, and knowledge of the terrain. So it was with crab fishermen from 1965 until 2005. Come one, come all. Bring your boats, your bait, and your deckhands and grab all you can.

The only limit was time. The National Marine Fisheries Service, federal regulators for the fishing industry under the National Oceanic and Atmospheric Administration, set up a crab season that ran only three to four days. Such a short span might seem wise as far as safety was concerned, since that would mean less time for accidents to occur, but it was actually the worst scenario possible. With such a tight window of opportunity and approximately 250 boats battling for the same catch, captains sometimes became reckless, ignoring hazardous conditions or other boats that had already staked out a spot.

"It was really intense," said Sig. "Phil and I would be right on top of each other, and he wasn't bashful about getting down and getting dirty. If he smelled crab in an area, he was going to jump in even if you were already there. He wasn't going to be polite about it. It was like pot for pot and let's go. That was okay with me. It was the name of the game."

Sig wasn't in a position to challenge Phil if he intruded into Sig's fishing area. Phil was ten years older and an established leader of the crab fleet.

"I'm not going to be on the radio barking at him," Sig said, "because he had more clout and had earned more respect. So I didn't say nothing."

But Sig showed little respect for the elements, his near-disastrous encounter with ice being only one of many hazardous trips he undertook.

"It could get really bad out there," he said. "Our last trip before the end of derby days was a three-day king crab season. The wind was blowing over seventy miles an hour the whole time, gusting up to ninety at times. Most of the other boats had to stop for a while. But I was dead set on getting my pots [down in the water]. It was just insane stupidity on my part. It took us two and a half hours to set twenty-five pots over a three-mile string, where normally that would take thirty minutes."

The difficulty was twofold: high winds and high waves.

"We couldn't make any headway," said Sig. "We'd plow over one wave and the next one was right down upon us. We were basically at a dead stop."

"Derby days was insane," said Thom Beers, creator and executive producer of *Deadliest Catch*. "I was up for thirty-six hours with those guys one time. It was nuts. It was so dramatic because the rule was, catch as much as you can until they tell you to stop. They'd cut each other's throats to get that crab."

Fishermen didn't literally kill one another, but the Bering Sea claimed many from their ranks during the forty-year span of derby days, with the mad dash considered a prime cause for the high number of fatalities. The Bering Sea Fishermen Memorial Page lists 196 deaths from the start of derby days in 1965 through its conclusion in January of 2005.

Concerns about the death rate contributed to the demise of derby days, but there were also worries about the damaging effects of over-fishing and environmental changes in the once crab-rich areas north of the Aleutian Islands.

In the early 1990s, more than 300 million pounds of snow crab were caught in the Bering Sea, earning fishermen $200 million. But by 1999, overfishing had devastated the crab population. To avoid the eventual extinction of crab in the Bering Sea, federal regulators severely limited their availability to fishermen. By 2004, snow crab season, previously measured in months, was cut to just five days. By 2005, the snow crab haul was down to 19.3 million pounds, worth $35 million.

"If you broke a [drive] shaft, or had a breakdown or an injury," Kale Garcia, owner of the crab boat *Aquila*, told the *High Country News*, "it could cost you your season."

Eventually, a quota system was implemented to replace derby days. But after the change was announced, there was still one last run by the full crab fleet beginning on January 13, 2005.

"This is it, the final one," Kevin Kaldestad, owner of nine fishing boats, told the *Anchorage Daily News* as his personal flotilla joined the last unencumbered hunt for crab. "We're all ready to get it over with safely and move on."

When he spoke of safety, Kaldestad did so in response to the pain of a horrible memory that had not dimmed in a decade. In 1995, his crab boat, the *Northwest Mariner*, facing forty-knot winds and twenty-four-foot waves, sank northwest of St. Paul Island. There were no survivors among the crew of six on board.

But Kaldestad's words about a safer future were quickly followed by a grim reminder of the disastrous past, affirmation of the need to phase out the Wild West days of crab fishing. The sinking of the *Big Valley* and the loss of deckhand Manu Lagai Jr. (swept off another crab boat, *Sultan*) both occurred in the first seventy-two hours of the last derby days.

When crab season resumed later that year, fishermen operated under the new system. The old method, TAC (total allowable catch), set a limit on the amount of crab that could be caught by the entire Bering fleet. Under the new rule, IFQ (individual fishing quota), each boat had its own quota.

And there were fewer boats to divide up the spoils because twenty-five of them, about 10 percent of the fleet, were removed from the competition through a $97 million federal buyout plan. The remaining boats had to account for that money through a tax.

The quota system is a catch-share program, similar to a cap-and-trade environmental plan. Begun in the 1970s in Iceland, New Zealand, and Australia, and successfully implemented in U.S. waters in the 1990s for halibut and black cod, the rule allows boat owners to buy a certain amount of quota, based on their catch totals in previous years, and fish for it, or they can sell or lease their quota to other boats while retaining a large chunk of the profits.

"This is going to help," said Kaldestad when the quota system was implemented. "It's not going to calm the ocean or make the crab come on board, but we can choose our window of opportunity, and we won't be racing anymore."

But the change didn't come without controversy. Some of the owners of the smaller boats felt they had been squeezed out of the market, and others resented the fact that some of the older boat owners could sell or lease their quotas and make a lot of money without lifting the anchor on their boats.

With the shift to the quota system, the number of boats fishing for red king crab dropped from 251 to 89 in one year. Those pursuing snow crab fell from 164 to 80.

For those left, however, the pace gradually became calmer. After four years, the snow crab season had stretched to more than seven months. The total allowable catch had also been moving back up, reaching 88.9 million pounds in the season just past, up 64 percent from the previous season's 54.3 million.

By knowing before they left port exactly how much crab they

could catch, boat owners could also engage in financial planning, a concept previously foreign to men who made their living at the whim of the sea.

Financial institutions loved it. "You know that a fisherman is going to be allocated *x* percent of the crab," banker Erik Olson told the *High Country News*. "You can translate that into dollars, and you can get a pretty good idea of what their revenue will be. That is a huge change. It's the difference between 'Grab a case of Red Bull, pray for good weather, and buckle up' and 'Now we have a business plan.'"

"As a younger guy I liked the derby days," Sig said. "At my age now, I'll take the quota system. That's only from a business perspective. If the weather gets so bad that you have to stop, you can. You can take a break if you need to shut her down. Before, you just wouldn't do it.

"Phil also learned to like the quota system because he could stop, but his fishing style didn't stop. He was still just as aggressive."

However, even with the switch to the quota system and ever-heightened safety measures, the number of fatalities has not dropped much. From 2005 until the spring of 2012, thirty-seven fishermen were lost. That's an average of more than four and a half a year. Under the derby days format, the rate of deaths was nearly five a year.

The Bering Sea is still the Bering Sea, and "the deadliest catch" is still an accurate description of crab fishing.

Helping to balance out the constant threat of death and disaster always hanging over a crab boat are the laughs, pranks, camaraderie, and the sight of pots full of crab emerging from the sea.

Whenever the talk about lost seamen and capsized ships got too heavy aboard his ship, Phil loved to break up the somber atmosphere by telling the story about the greenhorn who came on board his boat with his chest puffed out, bragging about how tough he was. He would talk about his days as a college quarterback, dismissing the idea of being overwhelmed by a rogue wave by saying it couldn't be any more fearsome than the gargantuan linemen who tried to overwhelm him on the football field.

When the *Cornelia Marie* left port with this cocky greenhorn, she encountered the usual hazardous conditions, winds as strong as sixty miles an hour, waves up to twenty-five feet high. To veteran deckhands, it was just normal working conditions.

Not to the quarterback. He raced up to the wheelhouse as if he'd just seen a ghost, fell on his hands and knees, and started crying, according to Phil.

"He said we were all going to die," Phil recalled. "He thought we were nuts. He wanted to go home. He expected me to call the Coast Guard."

Phil just looked at him with utter disdain and asked, "What is your problem?"

This photo of Phil was taken by Mike Lavallee in his shop one afternoon in Snohomish, Washington. Phil stopped in to say hello to Mike, who was tied up on the phone at the time. So Phil kicked back and lit up a cigarette. Mike says, "I got off the phone and walked into my outer office, where I found Phil sitting completely surrounded by smoke. I told him to not move an inch, and I went and grabbed my camera. It was amazing; the smoke was just hanging there, encircling him. I took about a dozen photos, and a few weeks later I showed them to Russ Herriott, Phil's manager and agent. Russ told me not to show them to anyone, and soon after that he called Phil to come in to look at them. When he saw this shot, Phil said, 'If I ever do a book I want *this* to be the cover photo.'"

LEFT: The F/V *American Eagle*, the crab boat on which Joe Wabey gave Phil his first shot at big-time crab fishing. Phil was so desperate to get on board that he volunteered to work for free.

RIGHT: Phil "Dirt" Harris at age twenty aboard the *American Eagle*.

Phil (right) and fellow deckhands sorting the crab.

LEFT: Mary, the beauty who caught Phil's eye. The gold nugget necklace was a gift from him. RIGHT: Phil and Mary enjoy a relaxing day. In this first picture taken of the couple, Phil was twenty-one and Mary was twenty-three.

Phil and Mary with her daughter, Meigon, two and a half years old.

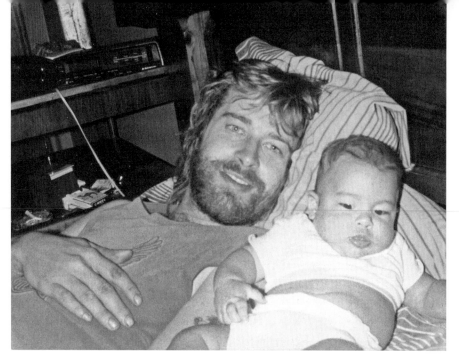

Phil with his firstborn son, Josh, at just three months.

Phil and Josh
in the wheelhouse.

Mary with two-and-a-half-year-
old Josh. At this time she was
pregnant with Jake.

LEFT: All the kids, left to right: Shane, Meigon, Jake (a few months old), and Josh.
RIGHT: Josh, almost three, with his little brother Jake, four months.

LEFT: Phil with Josh and Meigon at one of the many family outings Phil loved to coordinate. RIGHT: Jake, one and a half, and Josh, four—"Ding and Dong," as Phil sometimes affectionately referred to his boys in later years.

Captain Phil, twenty-nine, in the wheelhouse of the *Cornelia Marie*.

Captain Tony Lara, Phil's close friend, on deck aboard the *Cornelia Marie*. Tony is the man who knows the *Cornelia Marie* better than anyone.

The F/V *Cornelia Marie* in Dutch Harbor, Alaska. Phil and the crew are loading gear and stocking supplies for another crab fishing trip. Phil never left port on a Friday. He felt it was bad luck.

Phil on board the *Cornelia Marie* celebrating
another successful day of being "on the crab."

Phil petting Sammy and Precious, his Moluccan cockatoos.

Jake, age four, and Josh, age six, sitting on Santa's lap.

The world-famous Phil Harris birdhouse. Phil loved building these miniatures and gave each a distinctively different style and theme.

Phil and his father, Grant Harris. The time-honored tradition of the father-son fishing trip was well preserved in the Harris family.

Phil and Jake on board the *Cornelia Marie*. If Phil were still with us he would say of this photo, "I don't know if Jake is holding the crab or if the crab is holding Jake."

Phil with Russ Herriott in February 2008, after a charity auction dinner in Seattle. Dinner with Captain Phil went for a few thousand dollars that night to help a good cause. Phil said afterward, "Who the fuck would pay to have dinner with me?"

LEFT: Phil and Josh at an autograph session for some VIPs. Phil hated going to such sessions, but he always loved them once he was there. LOWER LEFT: Here Captain Phil is sitting in a different wheelhouse of sorts—behind a drum kit. He had been a drummer many years earlier, and one way or another he was destined to be a rock star. LOWER RIGHT: Phil flashes his infectious smile.

Phil with legendary motorcycle designer and master builder Dave Perewitz.

Phil, with his truck, chopper, and Harley. Long rides were his time away from the commotion of his newfound fame, when he got to be just Phil.

ABOVE: Phil and friends with NASCAR driver Greg Biffle (second from right) at Las Vegas Motor Speedway. The NASCAR track was where Phil and his fellow *Deadliest Catch* captains first realized the huge impact the show was going to have on their lives. When Phil, Sig Hansen, and Johnathan Hillstrand showed up at a race in 2007, everyone at the track that day—drivers included—knew they were in town. LEFT: A wonderful tribute to Phil, coordinated by our friends at the Rutledge Corn Maze in Tumwater, Washington. The picture was taken from about 2,000 feet.

Phil with Josh and Jake, pitching Monster Energy Drink in the Racegirl souvenir trailer at a NASCAR race in Fontana, California, September 2008.

Phil (back center), with Jake and Josh (front row, far left), visiting a classroom.

Jake, Josh, Phil, and Russ at a dinner in Las Vegas, after an appearance at the Super-cross Finals in May 2008.

Phil and his longtime good friend Dan Mittman, taking a break during one of their many motorcycle rides.

Phil loved kids, and he would stop at nothing to put a smile on their faces. Here he is sharing his wisdom with an elementary school class.

Jake and Josh with their mother, Mary.

LEFT: Jake, Mike Lavallee, and Josh at Phil's memorial at the Tulalip Casino north of Seattle. It was a sad day, but those in attendance were able to find some joy and laughter as they shared stories of Phil's amazing life. RIGHT: A beautiful and fitting tribute to Phil: the two urns containing Phil's ashes were Harley Davidson gas tanks, custom painted by his close friend Mike Lavallee to celebrate Phil's life on land (left) and at sea (right).

CHAPTER 11

DEADLIEST CATCH

If you're not taking a little bit of a risk, you're not living. If you're
not living on the edge, you're taking up too much space.

—*Sign on the wall in Thom Beers's office*

Thom Beers is very familiar with the edge. He has been living there
for a quarter century. Fascinated by those who flirt with danger and
death on a regular basis, whether for money, glory, research, or just
plain fun, he has made a very successful career out of showing these
true daredevils to the world in an ever-growing series of highly rated
reality shows.

To many viewers, the words "reality show" conjure up images of
American Idol and *Dancing with the Stars*. It is safe to say Thom will
never be found in a studio producing programs like that. Thom's idea
of a reality show is found outdoors, in the harsh climate of icy roads,
the lurking danger in wild jungles, and the stormy waters of the Bering Sea.

"He is the unchallenged king," wrote the *New York Times*, "of a
reality television form, variously known by names like 'macho TV' or
'testosterone reality,' that has swept across cable channels like a ratings-
driven wildfire."

Thom was producing such material in various forms long before
anyone had even coined the term "reality show."

While working for Turner Broadcasting and Paramount Syndicated Television for a dozen years, he produced specials with oceanic explorer Jacques Cousteau along with series like *National Geographic Explorer, Network Earth*, and shows like *Harley-Davidson: The American Motorcycle* and *The Incredible Life and Times of Robert L. Ripley, Believe It or Not.*

In 1997, Thom formed Original Productions to expand his vision of bringing stories of the wild and crazy to the screen. His company's shows have included *Ice Road Truckers, Ax Men, Black Gold, Swords: Life on the Line, Monster Garage, Biker Build-Off*, and *Backyard Nation*. He created a program entitled *Wild Things* that he described as "*National Geographic* meets *Cops*" and the show whose title best describes the ideal Thom Beers format: *1,000 Ways to Die*.

Original Productions currently has fourteen reality shows on the air and three more in preproduction. It has programs on seven networks, with at least one show on the air every night of the week.

But the program for which Thom is best known, the one that has elevated his reputation beyond all the others, is *Deadliest Catch*. Creator and executive producer of the show, Thom doesn't claim to be a genius who foresaw its potential from the beginning. Initially, it wasn't even a full program, just part of an agreement with the Discovery Channel to produce a two-hour special entitled *Extreme Alaska*.

Given a stack of possible material for the program, Thom started wading through it.

"I'm reading about musk oxen," he said, "mountain climbing, exploring dormant volcanos, all the insanity of Alaska."

Then Thom stopped, his eyes fixed on one article headlined "The Deadliest Job in the World." It was the world of crab fishing. He needed no more bait: he was hooked.

Having spent six years with Cousteau as his executive producer, sailing the world with him, Thom was already comfortable at sea when he headed for Dutch Harbor with a cameraman and soundman in January of 1999.

He would soon discover, however, that Jacques Cousteau and Phil Harris, though both men of the sea, lived in very different worlds.

"I figured I would talk my way onto a crab boat," said Thom.

That he did. He and his two-man crew got aboard the *Fierce Allegiance,* captained by Rick Mezich, for what was supposed to be a four-day trip.

"I felt like Gilligan," said Thom.

He felt a lot more like the most famous shipwreck victim in TV history shortly after the *Fierce Allegiance* entered the heart of the Bering Sea.

"Little did I know we were about to roll into the worst storm in that area in thirty years," Thom recalled.

Two hundred miles out at sea, the boat hit winds blowing at close to seventy knots with waves cresting at forty feet.

Welcome to the deadliest job in the world.

"It went way beyond seasickness," said Thom. "We all thought we were going to die."

What amazed him, impressing upon him from the start that he was in the company of men who redefined toughness, was that, while he and his two-man crew hung on like passengers on a runaway roller-coaster, praying it would stop, the boat's crew went about their business like it was just another day at the office, dropping pots, hauling them up, and sorting the crab.

The only effect the weather had on the boat's crew was to delay the return to port, providing an opportunity for two more days of fishing.

"These were hard-ass, hard-core guys," said Thom, who realized he had found Alaska at its most extreme in the waters far off the coast of the forty-ninth state. "Waves were blowing across the deck and crew members were getting swept in every direction except overboard. It was insanity."

Insanity that Thom and his own crew captured on camera, giddy at the thought of how good all this would look on screen.

By then, he didn't need any further assurance that he had found the macho men who could provide him with the next great reality show. Nevertheless, he found additional proof belowdecks when he went down to the galley.

It was about twenty minutes after a particularly rough wave had smashed into the boat. One of the deckhands had been injured by the torrent of water, hurled with such force that one of his legs had been torn open, blood everywhere.

Thom found the deckhand on the galley table, sewing up the deep gash with a needle and thread. All alone. No one to help him, nothing to deaden the pain.

"Dude," Thom told his cameraman, "we ain't in Kansas anymore. This is a whole new breed of guy."

The adrenaline flowing through him enabled Thom to shake off any apprehension he felt about the hazardous conditions and focus on the amazing sights and sounds before him.

It became a mantra for him as he kept telling himself and his cameraman, "Just get it on tape. Get it on tape. Get it on tape."

Thom had one camera that, on slow speed, could run for four hours.

He decided to tape it to the mast to get an aerial view of the deck and the sea beyond. With precision and ingenuity, he and his cameraman positioned the lens to get the ideal perspective and then securely fastened the camera to withstand whatever the angry sea might subject it to.

That was great, until the four hours was up and the camera had run out of tape. So Thom or his cameraman had to keep climbing back up that mast, struggling at times to hang on as the boat rocked violently.

"We had to do it even in the middle of storms," said Thom, "and I'm thinking, What the hell am I doing?"

While he and his cameraman were able to get the crowd-pleasing shots they wanted, pulling story lines out of the deckhands was not easy. There was no Phil Harris, Sig Hansen, or Johnathan Hillstrand in that first group.

"The crew of the *Fierce Allegiance* were not TV guys," said Thom. "They didn't have wise-ass personalities. They were just a bunch of hardworking guys."

Guys who didn't really get the concept that would grow into *Deadliest Catch*. Didn't really understand the potential for worldwide exposure.

At first, the deckhands just ignored Thom's group, paying attention to them only if they got in the way.

Determined to win the crew over, Thom did everything he could for them, from cooking their meals to doing their laundry, even helping pull crabs out of pots.

After the third day, he knew he was finally accepted. That day began with Thom crawling out of his bunk after a few precious hours of sleep, unable to straighten out his fingers. They were frozen in a condition referred to by crab fishermen as "the Claw."

It's very common for deckhands, after hours and hours of grabbing crabs out of pots in subzero temperatures, to find their hands are stuck in that gripping position, as if there were crabs still in their palms.

Normally, moving the hands around after rising, along with a warming sun on good days, loosens them up. Unaware of that, Thom, desperate for relief, was thrilled when a deckhand gave him a solution.

Uric acid, Thom was told. That's the best way to eliminate the stiffness.

Translation: urine.

Not about to turn down any suggestion that would allow him to grip a camera again, Thom walked out on deck, unzipped his fly, and proceeded to pee on his hands.

As he did so, he heard peals of laughter coming from above. Looking up, he saw the entire crew leaning on a railing, thoroughly enjoying the prank they had pulled.

Thom had become one of the guys.

As the trip stretched to a week, he and his film crew began to run out of cameras.

"We burned through all five we brought," he said. "Because of the saltwater, they were done. I started borrowing some of the guys' personal video cameras."

Thom even took the deck camera, used by the captain to constantly survey the ship.

"At the end, I had no alternative," he said. "Today, on these boats, we bring millions of dollars of technology. Back then, it was just me and two guys with nothing left at the end."

When he got back to Dutch Harbor, Thom realized he was fortunate just to be able to be back on solid ground, cameras or no cameras. The storm had taken seven lives from two boats, the *Lin-J* and the *Seawolf*.

The plan had been to spend just twelve minutes of the two-hour *Extreme Alaska* special on crab fishing.

But when Thom flew back home, he told officials at the Discovery Channel, "Look, there's something bigger here than just twelve minutes."

He got no argument from executives at Discovery. "Jaws were dropping every minute that segment was on," said Clark Bunting, former president and general manager of the channel. "It was hard to believe anybody does this for a living."

Thom got another sixty thousand dollars from Discovery, flew back to Alaska with more cameras and fresh ideas, and got enough material for a sixty-minute special.

It was called *The Deadliest Job in the World*.

"Like many of our reality shows," Thom said, "it was based on high stakes and high rewards in a really unique location."

The same could be said for Thom himself: high stakes and, as it turned out, a high reward.

"With no promotion," he recalled, "the show popped four million viewers, a massive number. It was the most lucrative show Discovery ever did."

Yet it took another three years before the decision was made by the network's officials to again dip their collective toes into the Bering Sea. In 2003, they commissioned Thom to head north once more, this time to produce a three-hour special.

Fortified with an enlarged film crew of six for the sequel, Thom, already knowing the kind of dramatic footage he could get, focused on finding some equally dramatic story lines to flesh out the show. The crew spread out, going to Seattle and Kodiak in addition to Dutch Harbor to find colorful captains to headline the program.

With around 250 boats in the Bering fleet back then, there were plenty to choose from.

"We had a real luxury when it came to casting," said Thom.

This time, he didn't have to do anybody's laundry to be accepted. Those in the crab industry had seen the one-hour special and the public's enthusiastic reaction to the material. They realized what being in the camera's eye could do for them.

"I think when you are in a position like Phil and all the other captains and you're out there alone in the Bering Sea," said Thom, "the water could pull you in one day and it would be like you never existed.

"So many people go through their whole lives, do a great job in whatever profession they are in, take care of their wives and kids, and then they're gone, merely a memory.

"But a good television show can immortalize you. It can allow you to make your mark in the world. That's especially true of crab boat captains. They are so damn heroic, rulers in their own little kingdom."

Of all the captains that Thom was interested in, only three or four turned him down.

He selected six boats for the special that would be called *America's Deadliest Season: Alaskan Crab Fishing*. Among the captains were Phil Harris and Sig Hansen.

Getting out onto the Bering Sea, Thom again found himself at odds with the elements, but for a very different reason.

Aboard the *Fierce Allegiance*, he had struggled in a storm far fiercer than he was prepared for. This time, looking forward to footage of fishermen battling driving rain and menacing waves, he found nothing but calm seas and mild weather.

One deckhand fell overboard, and his successful rescue, caught on camera, provided the ideal drama, terrifying danger with a happy ending.

"But the rest of the material was pretty mundane," said Thom.

That feeling was shared by the Discovery Channel hierarchy.

"This is not very good," Thom was told. "Not much excitement. No storms."

"I thought we were dead," he said.

Indeed, the Discovery Channel decided to bury the show. Plans were scrapped to break the program into three one-hour specials on consecutive Sunday nights. Instead, all three hours were aired in one block on a Sunday with no advance promotion. Not even a "Coming up next . . ."

According to Thom, the attitude was "Let's just get rid of it."

Back in 2003, a normal Sunday night rating for the Discovery Channel was a 0.8, as in 800,000 viewers. "That show started at point eight and went up every fifteen minutes," Thom said. "It went from eight hundred thousand to three point eight million in three hours.

"Crab fishing is made for TV, particularly when it's shot in Alaska in the winter, because there's very little sunlight. So it's dark and menacing, but, for contrast, you've got those beautiful sodium lights beaming down on the deck. Everything's wet, so you get that slick look. Everybody wears yellow and orange slickers that enhance the color, making the picture really vivid. It pops out at you. In the background, the Bering Sea trails off into blackness. It's almost like the crew is on a spaceship. They know if they get off, they are dead. They are in an extremely confined work space facing extraordinarily dangerous conditions."

It was a scene, said Thom, guaranteed to suck in viewers.

"The eye and the brain stuck to it," he said. "That's why those people kept watching. Nobody left."

Nothing gets a TV executive's attention like a few million viewers. The next day, Thom got a call from Billy Campbell, who had just that day become head of the Discovery Channel.

"Thom," Campbell said, "that was unbelievably exciting. I want more, fourteen, fifteen shows. How quickly can I get them?"

"About a year," Thom said.

"What? What do you mean a year?"

"Yeah," said Thom, "we'll shoot it next season."

"Screw the season," said Campbell, who was accustomed to working on scripted shows. "Just get a couple of boats out there."

"And do what?" asked Thom.

"Do whatever. We can't wait a year."

Ultimately, Campbell had no choice but to wait for the start of the next crab season, but his frustration quickly dissolved when *Deadliest Catch* debuted in 2005.

Even with the success of the earlier specials and the fame they had bestowed on the participating crab boat captains, they still weren't about to make life easier for the film crew that first season.

"None of the captains ever asked what they could do to help," said Thom. "The only thing they ever said was, 'Just stay the fuck out of our way.' We were dog meat on their boats, nothing but a pain in their ass."

As the seasons rolled by, however, that changed, as it has on Thom's other shows.

On the first season of *Ax Men*, Thom and his crew were filming a guy chopping down a tree. When the job was done, the cameraman said he needed to pause to change batteries. By the time he was done, the ax man was gone, off cutting another tree a quarter of a mile away without the slightest concern about the cameraman.

"By season two," said Thom, "I was the one changing batteries and the ax man says to me, 'Where do you want to go next? I was thinking about cutting down that tree over there. What do you think?'

"As soon as they get a sense of how many people are watching and how famous they are becoming, it all changes."

Still, the idea of having a camera constantly in their faces as they try to keep their boats on course, their crews alive, and their crab pots full causes different captains to react in different ways.

"Keith Colburn [captain of the *Wizard*] is still trying to throw our cameramen off the boat," Thom said. "He's thrown them out of the wheelhouse and off the deck. His favorite line is 'Get the fuck out of here or I'll kill you.'"

At first, Phil, too, had serious doubts about allowing a film crew on board, according to Jeff Conroy, the producer assigned to the *Cornelia Marie* in the show's first season.

"Well, what do I have to do?" he demanded of Jeff, now executive producer of *Deadliest Catch*.

"You don't have to do anything other than your job," Jeff told him. "I'll get what I need."

As Phil's apprehension began to melt, it was obvious to Jeff that this captain was going to be a star on the show.

"Phil was a producer's dream to work with," Jeff said, "because he had very little filter. He told the camera his whole life, warts and all."

"Once Phil learned to love the camera," agreed Thom, "he embraced the show. He was so bright with his observations and so funny with us.

"Phil was a military shell filled with testosterone. He'd make a lot of noise, but then, he'd back it up. He was a man's man."

"Phil didn't just live life," said Clark. "He grabbed life by the throat and shook it."

Not only did he have an appealing story to tell, but Phil learned to enhance it for the audience, creating even more drama than was inherently found in the hostile environment surrounding him.

"We would be looking at forty-foot waves," said Jeff, "and Phil, for the benefit of the camera, would say, 'Those are fucking sixty-foot waves. If they come over, they will bust these windows and could kill you.'

"We'd be walking around the deck and he'd say, 'You get in the way of those pots and they will crush you like a soda can.' He could be so dramatic that way and I loved it."

Jeff soon realized that behind the menacing warnings and the salty language was a master of the seas.

"The way he ran that boat was awe inspiring," said Jeff. "He was very much the skipper. I thought, It may be crazy out here in the Bering Sea, but I'm going to be all right with this guy. He knows what he's doing."

However, emboldened by his faith in the captain, Jeff soon abandoned caution.

"It's the same with nearly all my producers," he said. "When they first go out on the boat, most of their footage is shot from the vantage point of the shelter deck, the part of the ship protected from the sea. Everything is from that one angle because they stay where they're comfortable."

Not only are the huge waves intimidating, but, with pots swinging overhead and the deck moving violently at unpredictable angles, the shelter deck seems the only sane place to be.

"It's quite a lot to absorb," said Jeff. "But, as the days go by, the new producers and cameramen venture out farther and farther. Soon they are all over the boat like the seasoned guys."

Jeff himself went through that learning stage.

"I would start to tell myself, Okay, you can go two steps farther and not die," he said.

But Jeff soon went from fearful to foolhardy. Despite crashing waves and a restless sea one day, he wandered out to the edge of the deck, leaning on the railing.

"It's a mentality many producers and cameramen experience," Jeff said. "I wanted that awesome shot that completely douses me and the camera."

As a gigantic wave indeed engulfed him, he heard a loud, angry voice crackling over the loudspeaker from the wheelhouse.

"Jeff," screamed the voice, "get the fuck out of there!"

Recognizing it was Phil, Jeff didn't need to be told twice.

But later, he did need to be lectured a second time after "another instance of stupidity," as he put it. This one occurred one night with waves soaring over the *Cornelia Marie's* starboard side. Jeff noticed that the camera secured outside above the wheelhouse was not pointed in that direction.

Determined to capture the moment, Jeff climbed out onto a plankway that encircles the wheelhouse to turn the camera. Not only was it freezing outside, but the seas grew ever rougher, forcing him to struggle to secure his balance as he was repeatedly slapped in the face with wave after wave. Though the plankway was becoming slicker and his fingers were growing numb, Jeff managed to turn the camera.

But how was he going to get back inside? As his grip on the situation seemed to get more tenuous, he thought, So this is how I'm going to go. I didn't even need to do this. How dumb of me to be out here.

Jeff fell to his knees, gripped the plankway as tightly as he could, and crawled back around to the wheelhouse entrance, embarrassed at the thought of how he must look to any crabbers who might be watching but heartened by the realization that, most importantly, he was going to survive to see his wife and kids.

"Sometimes you get so excited about what you're doing as a filmmaker," said Jeff, "that you lose perspective."

With all they are confronted with, film crews hardly need another challenge, but they often get one nevertheless from deckhands who don't want them around. It's not just the captains who can be obstinate.

"In the beginning, a lot of the fishermen did not want to be on camera," Jeff said. "They saw no real benefit to us annoying the hell out of them. You're putting microphones on them and generally interfering with their job. If you want to do an interview, that might be five minutes they could be sleeping. And sleep is such a valuable commodity out there.

"The way the deckhands often see it, we are making a difficult job even more difficult."

Thom laughs at the idea that some scenes in *Deadliest Catch* are staged, an accusation leveled at other reality shows.

"You think Phil would have ever gone along with that? Never," said Thom. "There's no way any of the crab boat crews are directed to do anything. We pride ourselves on the authenticity of our show.

"A lot of programs at some of the smaller networks simply do not have the budget to make impactful television. If they only have two days to do an entire show, they may have to tell the people in front of the camera, 'Here's what you have to say.' The luxury we have is to be able to shoot four hundred hours for every hour that gets on TV. We have the time to develop authentic stories. You can see the difference between a show that is kind of fake and *Deadliest Catch*. That's why *Catch* wins Emmys."

On the crab boats, trying to waver from authenticity for even a few words can be a problem. If an engine starts sputtering loudly, a producer or cameraman may say to a captain, "Could you repeat what you just said?" But the reaction is often "Fuck you, I already said it."

"I know, but we didn't get it," the producer will insist.

"That's your problem, not mine," the captain will tell him.

The same might be said when it comes to danger at sea.

"Nobody mollycoddles our guys," said Thom. "But that's not necessary. They have been on those boats for so long, they're like part of the crew. Everybody is equally at risk."

While the focus of *Deadliest Catch* is the courage, work ethic, and daredevil nature of the fishermen, the same could be said for many of the cameramen who get the shots that captivate viewers. If maneuvering eight-hundred-pound pots along a slippery, gyrating deck into a menacing sea and then pulling them out, often under arctic conditions, is a scary way to make a living, how about the cameraman perched above the fishermen on a crane, hovering over that storm-tossed sea? How crazy is he?

Like the deckhands they shadow, *Deadliest Catch* cameramen have not always come home unscathed. Film crew members have suffered broken ribs and arms. Two have been airlifted off crab boats due to dehydration. "We have paid for two sets of new teeth," said Thom. "In both cases, our people did face-plants on the deck."

But that hasn't stopped them from stretching their limits.

"Nothing motivates a cameraman more than the possibility of winning an Emmy," said Thom. "*Deadliest Catch* has won several for cinematography. There's real competition over who can get the coolest shot.

"You are never going to see our cameramen working *The Biggest Loser* or *The Apprentice*. These are guys who just love adventure."

With more personnel and more cameras, the *Deadliest Catch* film crew has the whole boat adequately covered. Nothing that happens anywhere on board escapes the eye of the lens.

"When I was out there the first time," Thom said, "if a wave came over the ship, by the time you got the camera in place and pressed the record button, that wave was already gone."

While most cameramen on board are thinking about how an Emmy would look in their dens, there are a timid few who are more worried about making it back to their dens, their houses, and their families. Filming aboard a crab boat might have seemed like a great adventure when they were standing in Dutch Harbor, but the reality of standing on deck being buffeted by monster waves is quite another thing.

One cameraman, assigned to the *Aleutian Ballad,* used the satellite phone to call Jeff at the Original Productions studio in Burbank to complain after the sea became especially ferocious.

"Listen, man," the cameraman said, "it's not worth it for me to be out here for what I'm getting paid."

For *Deadliest Catch* producers, it's not worth having a cameraman on a crab boat if he doesn't want to work in rough seas.

"That's what makes the show," said Jeff. "It's TV gold for us. That's when we want our cameramen and producers to put off their sleep and film, film, film."

Jeff didn't argue with the disgruntled cameraman because he will never force an employee to put himself in harm's way.

"But it really burned me," he said, "because I always try to discourage people from doing this job before they ever get on a boat. I describe to them how miserable they are going to feel, how frustrated they are going to be because the harsh conditions will prevent them from being able to work as efficiently as they normally do, and how scared they are going to be because they will face danger to a degree they have never experienced before. I assure them that, no matter how much they're getting paid, they are going to feel like they are getting ripped off."

Finally, Jeff tells them, "If you're not willing to accept the fact that you are choosing to do something that could kill you, then don't go."

Before getting on a crab boat, every producer and cameraman is offered an airline ticket home from Dutch Harbor "with no questions asked," according to Jeff.

No one has yet taken him up on that offer.

"That's because, until they are out there, they don't believe it could be that bad," Jeff said.

The first sign that a cameraman realizes that it is indeed as bad as he was told and that he wishes he had taken the ticket home is a malfunctioning camera. Not one or two, but all of them. A cameraman will head down into the galley time and again, claiming his equipment isn't working. After the first few times, the producer realizes it is not the camera, but the cameraman who is breaking down.

"We had one cameraman who started to freak out after the boat was under way," said Thom. The cameraman's angst was increased when the boat caught fire. It returned to port, was repaired, and went out again, with the cameraman still on board. But then, the ship responded to a distress call from another crab boat, the *Big Valley*, as described earlier. Upon reaching the crisis site, the crew found the boat had sunk and there were bodies floating in the water.

"That was enough for that cameraman," Thom said. "He suffered a total meltdown. He announced, 'I'm done,' went into the room he was sleeping in, locked the door, and didn't come out for the remaining five days of the trip except to sneak some meals. The next time anyone saw him was when the boat was back in the harbor."

Early seasons or the current season, old equipment or new, it's never easy being on a crab boat film crew. "It's like one big cocktail of misery," said Jeff. "You suffer from sleep deprivation. At best, you get two to three hours in a row. The cold weather makes you constantly tired. Your whole world is moving in ways that you have never experienced before.

"Even a simple thing like walking down the steep, narrow steps to the galley to get a bottle of water could take fifteen minutes. You start thinking about anything else you might need down there because you certainly don't want to have to make that trip a second time.

"All these mental games require so much additional brain energy. When I talked to others in my film crew, I could see they were only operating on about eighty percent of their brainpower because they were so exhausted from just trying to function on the boat."

The realization of the effect the voyages were having on film crews caused Thom to order them to start calling in to the studio every twenty-four hours.

"We wanted to hear the story lines every day," he said, "what was happening on the boat, because, with the lack of sleep and the exhaustion, they get punch-drunk out there. They start to forget the stories they're tracking."

A reality show like *Deadliest Catch* costs between $400,000 and $600,000 an hour to produce. Much of that money goes to replacing equipment. Whether it's the cameras or monitors or the vast network of cable running through the ship, so much of it has to be thrown out at season's end because of the irreparable damage caused by seawater.

"We lose at least half a million dollars' worth of equipment every season," said Thom. "The minute we expose a camera to the Bering Sea, despite the fact we wrap it in gaffer's tape and bag it and do so many other things to protect it, we know that, ultimately, it will be fried."

Even items like computers can become casualties of the voyage, sent crashing to the floor by a boat-rocking wave.

Discovery Channel officials have tried to keep the budget relatively stable from season to season, but they have been receptive to paying for added elements when necessary. For example, Thom pushed for chase boats, vessels that would follow the crab boats in order to give the audience a view of the entire ship from the perspective of the sea.

"That's a big expense, running extra boats through a whole season," Thom said, "but I couldn't just rely on the happenstance of one boat going by another."

He also convinced Discovery to add helicopters for aerial views of the fleet.

"And with all that," said Thom, "I still haven't gotten the shot I've been looking for through the entire eight seasons the show has been on. I obtained the money to try for that shot twice, but I couldn't get it. It's the view of those balls of crab, a million of them, going across the ocean floor. I would love to see that. I've had cameras down there, but I still don't know how those crab travel along the bottom of the sea. Nobody does. Where are they going? Where do they come from?

"You ask the crab boat captains and they'll smile and tell you, 'We don't know. They just keep showing up.'"

Once it was established that crab fishing in the Bering Sea is extremely hard work under terribly dangerous conditions, that sometimes there are tons of crab to be found and sometimes there are none, there was a danger that constant repetition of the same routine, no matter how initially thrilling, would become a ratings killer.

So how did the producers advance the story? They turned to the people manning the boats and delved into their lives.

"*Catch* has always had the backdrop of extraordinary weather and extraordinary circumstances," said Clark Bunting, "but what has kept it on the air so long are extraordinary characters."

"The show went from a series about adventure on the high seas to a soap opera," said Thom. "I think it was the first soap opera for men. We've had the trials and tribulations of several deckhands struggling with drug issues or family issues, the disappearance of the father of *Northwestern* deckhand Jake Anderson, the pain of deckhands being separated from their families for long periods, the birth of the children of deckhands, and all sorts of other personal matters.

"We focus on the people willing to risk their lives in order to better their lives, to make more money than they ever dreamed of. That's really the essence of these shows."

Yet while it is the revolving cast of characters that has driven *Deadliest Catch* in recent years, Thom is amazed by the ongoing appeal of one lingering constant.

"I can't believe that, after eight seasons," he said, "when that crab pot comes up from the ocean, people are still fascinated by what's in it. How many times in each episode of each season does that pot come into view? Twenty? Yet viewers around the world still lean forward every time, as if they can beat the camera and get the first look. Their brains may tell them they've already seen this over and over and over again, but their hearts keep telling them there could be something in there they've never seen before."

And so, like the fishermen themselves, the viewers keep coming back to gaze into the dark waters of the most dangerous and unpredictable body of water on the planet.

CHAPTER 12

A STAR RISES IN THE NORTH

I'm just a fisherman. Why do people care?

— *Phil*

Something was wrong.

That was Hugh Gerrard's first thought on the day in 2005 that he got a call from Phil in Alaska. Hugh rarely heard from him when he was fishing.

But only a few words into the conversation, Hugh realized this call was about good news.

"He was so excited," said Hugh.

Phil had been selected for a role in a television show on Discovery Channel called *Deadliest Catch* and he thought it was the coolest thing ever.

"He told me I had to watch it," said Hugh.

When Phil came back home, he invited Hugh to lunch in Seattle. Phil gushed that he couldn't go anywhere without people asking for his autograph. He said that total strangers wanted to talk to him about "all kinds of wild shit."

Hugh could tell Phil was really into it. He loved the idea of becoming a celebrity.

When Phil and Hugh reached the restaurant, Phil predicted that at least ten people would approach him inside, asking him to sign something or to just give them a minute of his time. Phil sat there, anxiously eating and drinking while constantly turning his head, waiting for his audience to surround him. But not a single soul came up to the table.

Hugh laughed and laughed, rubbing it in while Phil sat there mystified and embarrassed.

Ultimately, however, Phil had the best laugh. That was the last public lunch he would enjoy without having to appease his adoring public. He didn't mind. He ate up the adulation.

Another close friend, Dan Mittman, got his first taste of Phil's sudden fame while sitting in an upscale Chicago bar. Dan hadn't seen *Deadliest Catch* yet and was getting his first look at the show when it flashed unexpectedly on a few screens in the bar.

As he watched, fascinated by the idea that a face and voice he'd known so well for so many years was suddenly up there, larger than life, on a big screen two thousand miles from home, he mentioned to a few of those on neighboring stools that he knew Phil, knew him very well. It might seem a bar like this, one catering to a Ferrari clientele, wouldn't be the kind of place where fishermen in the Bering Sea would make a big splash, but Dan quickly learned such seemingly logical thinking did not apply. As word spread about his personal connection, he was mobbed by people who wanted to know more about the instantly famous crab boat captain Phil Harris.

"They were really impressed by Phil," Dan said. "They were telling me, 'I wouldn't do that job. That guy is something else.'"

That day in that bar, Dan could see how his friend's life was about to change.

"I called Phil," Dan said, "and told him he was going to be a huge star. Phil had no clue."

Or perhaps he was still stung by the failure of those in that Seattle restaurant to recognize him.

"Naaaah. Fuck no," he told Dan. "I'm just a fuckin' fisherman."

It got harder and harder for Phil to stick to that line as his role on the show grew.

In Bothell, when he pulled his motorcycle up to the house of his old friend Joe Duvey, there was an autograph seeker who had somehow sniffed him out.

Trips to the Tulalip Casino north of Seattle had been outings that Phil and the old Bothell gang had loved to make together, but now they had to share him with his growing legion of fans.

"I couldn't believe it," said Jeff Sheets. "We'd be trying to play cards at the blackjack table and I'd notice people coming up behind us to stand next to Phil while a friend snapped a quick picture.

"Whenever we'd go out with him after he became famous, we'd see the fans coming after him. It was like watching a school of fish going after bait."

"Phil would be at an intersection," said Mike Crockett, another boyhood friend, "and a car would pull up and the driver would ask him to roll down the window for an autograph. We'd be riding motorcycles, stop for just a few seconds, and fans would surround him. Every time we'd go out on my boat, he'd do two live radio interviews while we were fishing. For him, the celebrity was constant, 24/7. He really enjoyed being recognized, even though he complained about it all the time."

Joe Wabey, the captain who gave Phil his first job on a boat, wasn't surprised that his former deckhand enjoyed becoming a major figure on *Deadliest Catch*.

"Phil always wanted to be a rock star," Joe said.

"I think, after all those years of fishing, it had become boring to him at times," said Russ Herriott, Phil's business manager, "but *Deadliest Catch* made it fun for him again."

Phil's doubts about remaining a crab fisherman, the role that most defined him, had begun to creep in when he reached his mid-forties. He would tell his friend Mike Crockett, "I don't want to go fishing anymore. I need to find some other way to make some money and be happy."

Phil tried to step back from crab fishing in the late '90s, but he didn't have a plan for what would come after. He talked about perhaps buying the RV dealership where Mike worked, but that was too foreign to the life he had known for so long.

"He wasn't sure what was next," said Mike, "but he felt he was truly done going north to Alaska."

Finally, Phil settled on the idea of buying a gillnetter boat and fishing for salmon off the Washington coast.

He bought a thirty-seven-footer anchored at Anacortes, seventy-eight miles north of Seattle near the Canadian border. He took his friend Joe Duvey up there, finalized the purchase, and the two of them began the voyage back down to Edmonds, just north of Seattle on Puget Sound.

It was dark when Phil and Joe headed out. Powered by a diesel motor mounted in its wooden frame, the boat couldn't go faster than seven knots. As it putt-putt-putted down the coast, Phil decided to spend the time housecleaning. Finding a full set of pots, pans, and dishes, he began tossing them overboard into the dark waters.

"We don't need any of this crap," he said. "We're not going to be doing any cooking. This is going to be a working boat."

All of a sudden, Phil started screaming. Joe figured it was because he had found still more cookware, but it was a lot more serious than that. Phil had discovered a fire radiating from the engine, located under the floorboards in the cabin.

"When he pulled off those floorboards," recalled Joe, "there were flames suddenly raging through the whole son-of-a-bitch boat."

The gillnetter was a mile offshore, a faint light flickering in the distance, growing ever brighter as the inferno spread.

"Fuck!" yelled Joe. "We're gonna die out here!"

"Bail me water!" screamed Phil. "Bail me water!"

Joe quickly complied, his terror sublimated to the task at hand. He plunged the few buckets he could find into the sea and then dashed to Phil, finding him with his face inches from the licking flames, coughing and gasping for breath.

After twenty minutes, Phil had extinguished the flames.

"I was scared to death," said Joe, "but he really fought that fire and saved our asses."

Having nearly lost his life saving the boat, Phil wasn't about to give it up. He enjoyed his leisurely fishing trips aboard the gillnetter, but that wasn't enough to make the living he had become accustomed to.

"My dad always told me to get out of fishing and go do something else," Josh said, "because he tried to get out for years and years. Along with the RV idea, he tried everything from selling boats to commercial real estate.

"He saw so many of his buddies give up fishing, but he never could. And now, as an adult, I see why. In all the other things he tried, the adrenaline just wasn't there, the feeling of freedom, the sense of being alive."

Nothing had worked as a replacement, so Phil stuck with crab fishing. But he remained ambivalent about it until 2004, when he was asked if cameras could be put on the *Cornelia Marie* for a new show debuting the following spring. Once the lights went on, Phil realized there was nowhere else on earth he would rather be.

While Phil bought into the idea of the show, he did so on his own terms. The character Tony Lara saw on *Deadliest Catch* was the same character he worked with for so many years aboard the *Cornelia Marie*, serving as Phil's relief skipper/engineer.

"I don't think he changed to be on television," Tony said. "A lot of the crap some of the other captains on there pull is just for the show, but that was never the case with Phil."

The idea that Phil or any crab fisherman would become an international celebrity was incomprehensible to his father, Grant, who worked in the Bering Sea back in an era when "glamorous" was the most unlikely word anybody would have used to describe his profession.

"When you do something much of your life," said Grant, "you don't think much about it. It's just something you do."

Once Phil got used to being in the spotlight, he learned to have fun with it.

One predawn morning, he and Mike were walking down a dock in Edmonds, Washington, heading for Mike's boat for a quiet, leisurely day of salmon fishing, one of Phil's forms of relaxation.

Even though it was still pitch dark and the surrounding lights offered little illumination, the owner of a boat on the other side of the dock was able to see enough of Phil to identify him.

"Hey," the man yelled out, "aren't you that guy on that show?"

"What are you talking about?" said Phil, playing dumb.

"You're that guy," the man insisted. "What's your name?"

"Bill," said Phil.

"No way," said the boat owner.

"Well, what's that guy like?" asked Phil. "Is he okay?"

"Yeah, he's a pretty cool dude," said the boat owner. "And you're him."

The man jumped into his boat, reappeared an instant later with a camera, and snapped a picture, leaving Phil to shake his head at the power of television.

Phil's appeal, especially among women, grew to proportions even he had trouble grasping. At first, he went bonkers when women began throwing themselves at him on a regular basis. In the early years of fame, he welcomed every available female fan into his bed, or her bed, or any free nook or cranny. And there was no shortage of volunteers who wanted to count Captain Phil as a conquest.

Women would approach him and blatantly ask the good captain if he'd like a blow job. Right then and there, on the spot. The rush included a ton of beautiful women, but in the long line of admirers were also gals of all shapes and ages.

Phil became accustomed to women lifting their shirts and asking him to sign an impressive boob. Some not only got inked with his distinctive signature but also received the Golden Ticket, his hotel room number, along with a time he could slot them in.

Because Dan had worked with several famous musicians, he knew the drill. So when he began accompanying Phil on some of his autograph sessions, it didn't take Dan long to realize his friend needed a crash course in Groupies 101.

For one thing, Phil was giving out his cell number like it was in the phone book. He didn't realize that, after the thrill of the encounter died down, he might not be so anxious to have these women bombarding his phone line 24/7.

Phil followed the same routine with his e-mail address. "He would give it out to random gorgeous chicks," Dan said. "But when his inbox was flooded with demands for attention, he'd be overwhelmed."

Phil soon realized he was going to have to do the unthinkable.

"I never thought I'd be in a position to be turning down so damned much beautiful pussy," he said, "but I just don't have the time. Ain't that a bitch?"

Even those Phil did have time for learned that intimacy with the captain didn't always mean full benefits. Mike Crockett remembers walking down a dock in Seattle with Phil and three of his companions from Texas, two male friends and a new girlfriend. Mike noticed the two men were wearing sharp jackets emblazoned with the *Cornelia Marie* logo.

"Wow," Mike said to Phil, pointing to the jackets, "those are really nice. I don't have one."

"Don't feel bad," Phil's girl told Mike, "I blow him and I don't have one either."

While strangers may have treated Phil with reverence, he didn't get that reaction from his old friends. Mike was amused when his wife,

Susan, a salesperson for a wine company, informed him that she was one of a select group of employees to win the organization's grand sales prize: a dinner at a fancy downtown Seattle restaurant with . . . Captain Phil.

"Dude," Mike told Phil, "you're attending this dinner in downtown Seattle with people from the wine industry."

"I am?" said Phil.

"You are," said Mike. "And I'm going to be there."

"Why?"

"Because Susan won a dinner with you."

The fact that a company would consider dinner with him to be a grand prize was beyond Phil's comprehension.

But no matter the occasion, he was never shy about living up to his image. While the other five couples sat at the dinner table, buzzing about their upcoming meeting with the famous sea captain, Mike and Susan remained quiet.

When Phil finally arrived—late, of course—he headed straight for Mike, gave him a big hug, and proclaimed loudly, "Fuck, oh dear, I can't believe you're here."

That was the Phil the others had all come to see.

"It was really strange," said Mike, "to be sitting in a room with ten people you don't know who are all so excited about meeting this famous guy and in walks your fishing buddy."

"I never treated him any differently," Jeff said. "To me, he was just Phil, still wearing his T-shirt, Levi's, and cowboy boots."

And that's the way he was determined to stay. "I'm not going to be any different," Phil kept telling family and friends, worried that the fame and fortune might turn him into somebody he wouldn't like.

The key, he felt, was keeping it all in perspective.

"I'm one of the luckiest guys alive," he said, "to be able to not only fish, but to have the notoriety that comes with it. I didn't ask for it, I wasn't looking for it, and someday this will all be behind me and I'll be the same guy I've always been, just plain Phil."

If Phil occasionally strayed from that perspective, the Bothell gang was there to pull him back.

"When he'd start to act like Hollywood, we'd call him on it," said Jeff.

While Phil's friends may not have been able to relate to his celebrity status, they didn't dispute the image they saw on TV.

"To us," said Jeff, "he was always this bigger-than-life kind of guy who lived fast and hard."

Those who saw him only on the tube or at a distance might have thought all his fame meant to him was a lot of crazy nights and wild sex. They would have been wrong.

While it was harder for Phil to carve out time for his old friends because of the many demands of his burgeoning public life, when Jeff's wife, Michelle, was diagnosed with cancer, Phil was there.

"He made it a point to come by the house to see her, or at least call, every time he was in town," Jeff said.

When Michelle's condition worsened, Phil visited her at the hospital before heading up for what would turn out to be his last fishing trip. Michelle died in October of 2009, four months before Phil's own passing.

Phil spent much of his time on land making charitable appearances. His schedule, though, was such a whirlwind that sometimes he didn't know his destination even while en route there.

"What are we doing?" he asked Russ one time after boarding a plane.

"We're going to a retirement home."

"Why do I want to do that?"

"You're already in the air, so you've got no choice," Russ replied. "Besides," he added, "it's good karma. You and I are going to be there one day with somebody sponge bathing us."

The organizers of the event were expecting 125 to 150 paid customers for a dinner honoring Phil. They had to switch to a much larger venue when 375 people ordered tickets.

They could have sold still more, but heavy ticket demand at the end left no time to relocate to a still bigger venue.

At the end of the evening, Phil and Russ were heading up a flight of stairs toward an exit when Phil stopped and, looking back down, saw a segment of the crowd still lingering below.

"We can't leave," he told Russ. "There are still people down there who want to meet me and get an autograph. I don't want to let them down."

"You're kidding, right?" said Russ.

"No, let's go back."

The pair returned, the receiving table was set back up, and Phil sat there for an additional two and a half hours.

"He wasn't one to sign a quick autograph and good-bye," Russ said. "Every one was accompanied by a minimum of forty-five to sixty seconds of exchanging pleasantries. Then another minute and another minute. He wanted the person to feel comfortable. That was the real Phil.

"What people saw on the outside on TV didn't tell you what was on the inside. Yes, he had that look. The guy was everything you would expect a crab captain to be—grungy, foulmouthed, and generally disgusting. His gruff exterior included the harsh voice, tattoos, and cutoff shorts. But, when you got to know him, you discovered a gooey chocolate center."

His appeal may have been obvious to his fans and to Russ, but Phil himself remained as puzzled about the effect he had on people as he was the first time he was recognized.

On one occasion, he and Russ spent six hours at an appearance at a grocery store outside Seattle to promote Phil's brand of coffee, drawing a crowd of around a thousand.

Russ drove Phil's Corvette on the trip back to Seattle while Phil sat in the passenger seat with a Red Bull.

"I don't get it," he told Russ.

"Get what?" asked Russ.

"Why were they standing in a long line to get my signature?" said Phil. "After all this time, I still don't understand it."

"You go into people's living rooms one night a week," Russ replied. "And somehow, some way, you've created a connection with them. Your personality, the way you speak, the way you act. They see you raising your boys on TV. How you deal with them. Parents relate to that.

"You've got to understand something. Maybe it will scare you, but you impact people's lives. So how you behave when you meet them is important. If you receive them coldly, then they'll think you're an asshole. If you receive them warmly, like you did with those people today, they are going to go home, watch the show, and feel like you are their friend."

Although Russ himself became good friends with Phil, their relationship began as a mutually beneficial business arrangement. In the summer of 2006, as the ratings for *Deadliest Catch* began to rise, and Phil's visibility along with it, he started to listen to people who told him his rapidly growing fame should translate into fortune.

To make that happen, Phil knew he was going to need a business manager and a lawyer.

First, the manager. Phil's favorite sport was auto racing, so that offered him a comfort zone in which to explore his options. When he found Russ, who was running a sports and entertainment marketing management company, Phil searched no further.

"We forged a friendship over the phone when he first called me," said Russ. "He wanted advice. I flew up to Seattle in November of 2006 and he picked me up at the airport. I had no idea what I was getting into with this guy."

Nobody joins Phil's inner circle without going through initiation rites. In Russ's case, Phil wasted no time.

"He and Sig and some other guys took me out to dinner and got me trashed," Russ said. "I was drinking Jack and Coke, Red Bull and vodka. Finally, they brought out the duck farts [whiskey, amaretto, and

Bailey's Irish Cream, a Phil favorite]. I was ripped all night long and they thought, Hey, this guy's all right."

Then it was time to talk business.

"Phil wanted to know how the TV/entertainment business works," Russ said, "so I kind of gave him the dime tour with respect to talent fees, his rights, merchandising, licensing, and endorsements. I also floated some ideas about what could be done with the *Cornelia Marie*.

"I stressed that there was a lot more to it than just 'Hey, I'm Captain Phil Harris and you should go to so-and-so auto dealership.' I compared it to NASCAR and Indy racing, showing him how the drivers, teams, and sponsors all make money. The possibilities for crab fishing, I said, were roughly the same."

Russ figured the best way for Phil to see the parallels between his profession and his obsession as a sports fan was to take him to some races. Russ brought him to a NASCAR event in Las Vegas in March of 2007 where Phil met an icon of the sport, Tony Stewart, who became a good friend.

Phil subsequently called Tony to wish him luck before a race and he won. A ritual was born. Tony insisted on a Phil Harris call before every race. Tony even joked that he was going to pay for a satellite phone on the *Cornelia Marie* so that, even when Phil was fishing, he could make the prerace call.

Tony didn't have an exclusive hot line to Phil, though. Greg Biffle, another driver, also became a friend and a recipient of those lucky calls. When one of them was followed by a first-place finish for Greg, Phil bragged to anyone who would listen, "That was me, man. I won the race for him."

In May of 2007, the connection between the crab boats and the race cars went public when Russ arranged for Phil to take fellow captains Sig Hansen and Johnathan Hillstrand, along with Phil's dad, Grant, to Charlotte for the Coca-Cola 600.

"That's when it really clicked that these guys were something special," Russ said. "We were standing down in the pit area on a Thursday before cup qualifying when one of the photographers shooting the cars saw our group. 'Hey,' he yelled, 'those are the guys from *Deadliest Catch*.' All the other photographers turned and started snapping shots of Phil Sig, and Johnathan. Then many of the drivers spotted the three captains and came over to meet them."

At the Charlotte airport on the way home, the group was approached by a couple from New Zealand.

"When your show comes on where we live," they told Phil and his companions, "everything comes to a halt."

"That trip," said Russ, "got Sig and Johnathan thinking, 'Hey, we've got something here.' So they went out and got their own management."

"After we had been on the show for a year," said Keith Colburn, captain of the *Wizard*, "the novelty had worn off. As captains, we were all more interested in how we could capitalize on the opportunity. As a result, the interaction between all of us became a little strained. We were not only competing for crab, but for endorsements and appearances as well."

Working within the parameters of what the Discovery Channel allows the individual captains to generate in terms of outside income tied to their roles on *Deadliest Catch*, Russ and Phil first signed an endorsement deal with a manufacturer of winches for crab boats.

"After that," Russ said, "we took advantage of everything we could, whether it was starting a coffee company or striking a deal with a beer company.

"The Discovery contracts were pretty rigid. They didn't give us a lot of opportunities, and I understand and respect why Discovery does that. They need to protect their brand. But to this day, it's still a burr under my saddle that we didn't get a chance to take advantage of all the endorsements and all the publicity we could have had because of Phil's exposure on the show."

Just as Phil poured all of his emotions into his role as captain, he did the same with his celebrity status. And it wasn't always pretty.

Russ worked on one endorsement deal that seemed promising, but there were still problems to be worked out. He made the mistake of telling Phil about it before a contract was signed.

Hearing only the positive side of the proposal while ignoring the negatives, Phil bragged to friends about his new sponsor and all the money he was going to get. Instead, the deal collapsed.

"When I would tell him a deal had fallen apart," said Russ, "he would just stare at me while sliding down in his seat."

Phil had definite ideas about his business activities, and they didn't always coincide with Russ's game plan. The result was ongoing friction that often seemed to leave Russ with one foot out the door.

It's hard to say what was greater, the number of times Phil fired Russ or the number of times Russ quit. Sometimes, Phil would yell, "You're fired!" and Russ would respond, "Too late, I already quit."

It was like New York Yankees owner George Steinbrenner and manager Billy Martin. Steinbrenner hired and fired Martin five times. Phil and Russ exceeded that total, but, their friendship always remaining intact, they would soon get back to business.

Along with Russ, Phil needed a lawyer for his contract negotiations. As with everything else he did, he had a unique modus operandi when it came to hiring people.

The first time he saw Ed Ritter, a young, eager Seattle attorney, it was in 2008 in a courtroom in Monroe, Washington, near Phil's Lake Stevens home.

Actually, it was Ed who first spotted Phil. The lawyer was in the courtroom to take care of some paperwork for his firm, but the room was empty when he arrived. Except, that is, for a rough-looking customer sitting all alone off in one corner.

A huge fan of *Deadliest Catch*, Ed was almost certain it was the famous Captain Phil Harris.

I'm going to go up and say hi to him, Ed thought. The worst he can do is punch me in the face.

Hesitantly, Ed approached Phil and asked, "Are you who I think you are?"

Phil turned a searing glare on the man standing in front of him in a three-piece suit, and, instead of responding to the question, asked one of his own: "Are you a lawyer?"

"Yes," was all Ed said. It was all he had time to say. Once he replied in the affirmative, Phil jumped up, got a firm grip on Ed's vest, and dragged him out into an adjacent hallway.

While the startled Ed tried to smooth out his disheveled clothes, Phil said, "I need a good lawyer to get rid of these tickets. A good lawyer will go in there and get them dismissed. So, are you a good lawyer?"

Phil didn't like having a license plate on the front of his Corvette, so he removed it, figuring the one on the back was sufficient. When he was stopped for driving at his usual pace, meaning above the speed limit, he had been given two tickets, one for the missing plate and one for speeding.

Familiar as Phil was to him, Ed was still intimidated by the large and demanding figure in front of him. Nervously, Ed told Phil that he thought he could handle the situation.

"Okay, do it," said Phil, "and after that, we'll talk."

Ed marched back into the courtroom and, when the judge arrived, the lawyer got the charges dismissed on a technicality after spotting an irregularity in the way the police officer had filled out the tickets.

Feeling pretty good about himself, Ed marched back out to the hallway, his look of intimidation replaced with one of confidence.

"Got it done," he said with a smile.

Surely that would calm Phil down.

Not exactly. Again he grabbed a chunk of Ed's vest and, this time, dragged the attorney down the hallway and out to the parking lot.

"All right, you're my guy," Phil said. "Any kind of legal work, I'm coming to you."

Ed was so excited about being connected to someone he regularly saw on TV that he told Phil he'd work for free. But deep down, although Ed gave Phil his phone number, he figured he would never see Phil again.

That night, Ed's phone rang. It was Phil.

"What're you doing?" he asked.

"Just sitting here at home with my wife," said Ed.

"Where do you live?"

Phil came over and spent three hours at Ed's house. Brenda, Ed's wife, couldn't believe this star was actually in her living room sitting next to the TV on which he appeared weekly. Both of the Ritters quickly realized the guy they saw on the tube was just a character on a program.

"The TV show made Phil look like a big, burly, mean kind of guy," Ed said, "someone you couldn't approach. In reality, he was just as nice as can be. No bragging, very humble."

For the first year of their relationship, Ed, as he had promised, worked for nothing. He wasn't concerned because, as he had hoped, he wound up profiting anyway by getting involved in some of Phil's growing business concerns and through the many others Phil sent Ed's way. Then, after the first year, Phil directed his bookkeeper to call Ed's office to find out how much Phil would have owed had Ed been charging his normal rate. Phil then sent a check for that amount.

While Russ and Ed both loved working with Phil, they knew they were constantly battling his limited attention span.

"When I talked about anything legal with Phil," Ed said, "he'd usually be sitting in a chair. As I started to explain some business matter to him, he would begin to slide down and his eyes would roll to the back of his head. You only had a five-minute window to talk about what you needed to discuss. That was it. Then he was gone mentally. There were a number of times when he fell asleep while I was talking to him about some legal issue for which I needed his approval. He'd start snoring and I'd have to lean across the table and shake him."

Russ, too, knew the drill. "When I got him on the phone to talk business, it was only for ninety seconds," Russ said. "You could measure it with an egg timer. You had to get everything in as fast as you could, because, after a minute and a half, his attention had been exhausted.

"Like clockwork, he would come up with the same old excuse. 'I gotta go,' Phil would tell me. 'There's a cop behind me. I'm going to get pulled over. I'll call you later.'"

He would never call back.

"It got to be a joke," said Russ. "When I would get hold of him on a plane, he would say, 'Can't talk. A cop just pulled up behind me.'"

Ed and Russ just laughed it off. They, like everybody else from his shipmates to his multitude of fans around the world, were charmed by Phil.

"He had charisma," said Tony Lara, who sailed with Phil for many years. "He had that goofy little giggle and a way about him that everybody seemed to like no matter what he did or said."

Tony saw that firsthand in an incident that still has him shaking his head years later. He and Phil had gone into a marine supply store in Dutch Harbor.

"They had messed up an order we had placed," Tony said.

The manager, a woman, came over to explain what had happened. Phil didn't want to listen, preferring instead to blast the lady verbally. He called her a bitch, and that was the nicest word he used in a string of expletives.

"I was so embarrassed that I covered my head," Tony said.

Finally, Phil stormed out to smoke a cigarette.

That left Tony alone with the manager. Looking out the window at Phil, she said, in all seriousness, "Isn't he just the nicest guy?"

Tony was flabbergasted.

"What did I just miss?" he wondered. "If I had said all that and behaved like that, they would have thrown me in jail."

Not Phil.

"Some people have got it," said Tony, "and some people don't. Phil had it."

Phil Harris, ever the rock star.

CHAPTER 13

A WARNING SHOT

I've never been that close to death.

—Phil

For most of his life, Phil Harris charted his own course. Undaunted by laws, untouched by fear, unimpressed by cautionary tales, he followed his inner compass, plowing through the harsh elements of both the Bering Sea and everyday life seemingly without concern.

He was a crab boat captain.

He was a father.

He was a womanizer.

He was a chain-smoker, an alcoholic, a drug user, a fast and furious lover of cars and motorcycles, and a man with eating habits that would make Michelle Obama cringe.

But Phil made no apologies for his lifestyle. Instead he justified it by portraying his vices as virtues.

As Phil slid into middle age, the wild urges of his youth still tugged at him. Johnathan Hillstrand, co-captain of the *Time Bandit* along with his brother Andy, still laughs about the time he and Phil were speeding down a highway after both had become *Deadliest Catch* stars.

"He was the only guy I know who would pass me a cigarette when we're doin' a hundred miles an hour on our Harleys," said Johnathan.

"I wasn't even thinking about smoking a damned cigarette, but here came Phil, easing over while saying, 'Here, dude.'

"For the longest time, I wondered how the hell he got it lit. Turned out, he'd installed a lighter on his bike."

On one occasion, Phil, accompanied by the Hillstrands, came to L.A. for a five-day visit. While in town, Phil contacted *Deadliest Catch* producer Thom Beers, whose studios are in Burbank. Knowing the fishing trio hadn't rented a car, and in possession of a fleet of vehicles from his *Monster Garage* reality show, Thom offered Phil a '96 Chevy Impala Super Sport.

He didn't have to offer twice. Off the group raced, and Thom didn't hear from them over the next four days. Then, finally, he got a call from Phil.

"Hey, Thom," Phil said, "we had to leave town in a hurry. Would you mind getting someone to pick up your car?"

"Not a problem," said Thom. "Where is it?"

"Uh . . . it's at the Sahara in Vegas."

When Thom got the car back, he found tar in the form of footprints on all the windows, as if somebody had been walking on them.

He couldn't imagine what the three captains had been doing, and he never asked.

The good times continued to roll for Phil even as his sons entered adulthood and developed a wild streak of their own. Both had joined him on the *Cornelia Marie*—Josh starting in 2001, Jake four years later. Phil was keenly aware that turning his sons into crab fishermen, subjecting them to the stress inherent in the job, could push them into addiction as well. Phil wanted to steer them down a different path. And he thought he could do so, without reforming to become a role model, by alleviating some of the pressures of crab fishing, especially for the younger, smaller Jake.

Remembering the lack of respect he had encountered as the

captain's son on the *Golden Viking,* Phil wanted to spare Jake that indignity when he came on board the *Cornelia Marie.* So Phil made it clear to everyone that Jake was working for the deck boss and would not, under any circumstances, go over the boss's head to get a favor from Daddy.

Still, Phil wanted the crew to know that, despite his five-foot-eight, 145-pound frame, Jake was one tough kid. And to prove his point, Phil loved to tell the story about the game of chicken he had played with his younger son when Jake was a rebellious teenager.

It was a common game in the bars of Dutch Harbor. Two crabbers would put their forearms side by side, skin on skin, while a third would drop a lit cigarette between them. The man who flinched first was the loser, the weaker man in the eyes of his peers.

That was the test Phil challenged Jake to take. And, as Phil told his crew with pride in his voice, it was he, not Jake, who had flinched first.

But as much as Phil tried to protect Jake and Josh from the intensity of life on the Bering Sea, they sank more and more into a drunken state as they grew older and entered their twenties.

"We were the ones partying all the time," said Josh, "totally out of control."

How could they have turned out any other way after watching their father stagger through outrageous incident after outrageous incident for years without suffering for it? Because Phil was surrounded by enablers, there were rarely any consequences for his actions.

For example, at a house party he threw, Phil, having already had too much to drink, lurched out of the house, saying to no one in particular, "We need to go get some more beer." He hopped into his truck parked in front of his house, told Josh and a few of his buddies to jump into the bed of the vehicle, jammed it into reverse, and crashed right into an arriving guest's new Camaro.

Out stepped one of Phil's friends, six-foot-six with a frame like a bodybuilder.

"This guy was massive, one of the biggest men I've ever seen in my life," said Josh.

He calmly walked over to the truck and, in a voice as threatening as his appearance, said, "I just bought this car three hours ago, Phil."

The look on Phil's face went from menacing to meek.

"Are you going to kick my ass?" he asked, looking up at the hulk standing in front of his window.

"N-a-a-w," was the reply. "We'll just say I got hit at the grocery store."

Party on.

Josh remembers driving down a Bothell street one day with his dad when Phil suddenly pulled over to the curb and told his son to stay in the car.

He then jumped out and intercepted a man walking down the street. The two started talking in front of a liquor store that had a large window looking out on the street. The conversation became more animated, especially on Phil's side. Finally he stopped, tilted his head for an instant at a weird angle, grabbed the man, and threw him through the window into the store.

Phil then calmly marched back to the car, got in, looked at Josh, and said, "Motherfucker owed me some money."

By then, a woman from the store was out in the street, screaming at Phil.

"Might get in some trouble for this one," he said as he hit the accelerator and took off.

The police indeed came to Phil's house and lectured him, but that was the end of it.

Again, no consequences.

No immediate consequences. But as Phil saw Jake and Josh emulating his behavior, even he began to doubt his lifestyle. The problem, Phil realized, wasn't the crab fishing. It was him.

"Once he started to see the effect he had on us," said Josh, "he changed."

Phil realized that, for him, it was time for the party to be over. His resolution to tone down his wild ways coincided with his decision to remove Teresa from his life, which made the transition much easier. The final years of his relationship with Teresa had been long and emotionally taxing, but when Phil finally split, the elation that overwhelmed him wiped away all the fears and negative thoughts. His dread about the financial cost of divorcing her was gone, along with the shackles of his suffocating second marriage. His ongoing success at sea would keep him afloat and still prosperous.

His close friend Dan Mittman invited Phil to move into the new home Dan had recently purchased on a scenic parcel of land outside Seattle. Phil appreciated the offer but declined, zestfully proclaiming, "This is the first time in my life I'm totally free."

What would he do with the freedom? Having already enjoyed spaciousness and luxury in the home he shared with Teresa on Echo Lake Road in Snohomish, Washington, a home that included a waterfall and a pond, Phil decided that a simpler lifestyle was a better fit for him at that point in his life. After so many years in his captain's quarters with anything he needed within arm's reach, he felt a fifth-wheel recreational vehicle would be an ideal counterpart on land.

He bought a massive, luxurious motor home that set him back nearly two hundred grand and featured granite countertops, a fireplace, and granite steps leading up to his bedroom. Phil also purchased two lots in Lake Conner Park, a private camping club located in the city of Lake Stevens thirty-six miles northeast of Seattle.

"He didn't need to impress anybody," said Jake, "so he got a place he really liked."

With sixty-foot trees looming over the park, moss and ferns dominating the surrounding foliage, spectacular views of the lake from every slice of property, and an abundance of wildlife roaming the area—from deer to cougars to bears—Phil felt he had finally found a haven from his hectic life. It was the perfect place to recharge when he was about to be overwhelmed by stress. Nobody had to remind him that he was in his late forties. There were days when he felt twenty years older, the mileage piling up on a man who had been in the fast lane since his teens.

At the entryway to his fifth wheel, partially shielded from inquisitive eyes by a hedge, Phil placed an imposing suit of armor to stand guard.

Anyone looking inside would have no doubts about who lived there. Pictures of Phil with celebrities and with his boys were plentiful. NASCAR racing memorabilia were everywhere. The closet was jammed with Harley clothing, and his trademark cowboy boots were parked by the coffee table, ready for action.

Next to the trailer, he built a gazebo and installed intricate decking around the fifth wheel. As he explained to visitors, "I need the deck so I can ride my bike right up to the fucking door."

Phil no longer needed a refuge in the backyard to escape Teresa's wrath. But by now, building his birdhouses, the excuse he'd used to disappear out there, had become a treasured hobby. So he constructed a toolshed on the Lake Connor property in which he kept turning out his mini masterpieces.

Phil also put in a platform for his Bayliner cruise boat and a carport for the designer golf cart with chrome mag wheels that he used to putter around the park.

"To me, it was like a little mansion," said Jake. "It was really quiet out there. Nobody fucked with him. He just chilled with his motorcycle, his dog, his golf cart, his boat, and his birdhouses."

"When he came home from a fishing trip," said Lynn Andrews, Phil's personal assistant, "he just wanted to turn the world off. He sat in front of his fireplace, turned up the heat as high as he could, smoked, and watched TV."

But it wasn't always quiet and peaceful around Phil's lair. One night, Lynn, with Phil gone for the evening, was engaged in the never-ending task of cleaning up the mess her boss had left behind. As always, she kept the front door open to counteract the stifling tempera-ture generated by the heater and the fireplace.

She would toss the trash onto the front deck and then scoop it up and dispose of it when she left.

On this night, Lynn heard rustling sounds coming from outside. Figuring Phil had returned early, she went to the front door only to discover a bear on the porch, munching on a piece of salmon.

"I was completely freaked out," said Lynn, remembering how she slammed the door and hunkered down inside, afraid to venture out into the dark park.

Close to midnight, she heard Phil pull up.

"What are you still doing here?" he asked when he found Lynn inside.

"I didn't want to get eaten on my way to my car," she said after tell-ing him about the unwelcome visitor.

"Oh," said Phil, "so you just waited for me, figuring he would get me on the way in."

After adding his trademark giggle, he walked Lynn to her car. Once again, this grizzly had shown that, deep down, he was just a teddy bear.

But with Phil, it seemed, there was always another side. Lynn might not have thought of him as being so warm and protecting if she had known it was no accident that the bear was prowling around. Ever mischievous, Phil deliberately left fish outside in order to lure bears so he could watch them strut and growl.

While his neighbors respected Phil's privacy, snooping fans were not as considerate. They would drive through the park and pause at the famous fifth wheel, trying to get a glimpse over the hedge of the captain in his natural habitat, like tourists on a Hollywood tour of the homes of the stars. One overzealous fan pounded on Phil's door at six in the morning, demanding to shake his hand. What he got instead was a shaking fist.

Phil's invited guests got a lot more. In case they decided to spend a few days with him, he installed another massive fifth wheel on his next-door lot.

By 2008, at the peak of his fame at fifty-one, Phil finally seemed at peace with himself, whether in Lake Connor or still reigning as the master of the Bering Sea.

But while he appeared to be sailing on calm waters, inside him a storm was brewing, fueled by decades of self-destructive behavior.

When it came to the surface, it didn't seem that serious at first. Phil had been experiencing aches in his legs for a while due to a minor design flaw in the *Cornelia Marie*. The configuration of the wheelhouse makes it difficult for the man in control to stand up. His knees would be pinned between the bolted-down chair and the control panel. Sitting is much easier, but over a prolonged period it can be hard on the legs.

What might have been nothing more than an irritating inconvenience for someone else soon grew into a potentially deadly situation for Phil, worse than any wave he ever faced. He developed blood clots in his knees from sitting in that chair day after day, month after month, year after year.

Of course, it didn't help that, while he was sitting there, he puffed away on pack after pack of cigarettes. Phil could go through five packs a day. His record was eight.

Add the drug addiction, alcoholism, and a lifetime of eating junk food, and it's hardly surprising that his body wore out prematurely.

The blood clots spread to Phil's lungs, causing a pulmonary embolism.

He was at sea when he was stricken. When he began coughing up blood, he refused to head to land for treatment. He tried to rationalize his condition by insisting he was merely suffering the aftereffects of a rib cage injury he had suffered a few days earlier when a powerful wave had banged him into the side of the wheelhouse. It was going to take more than a little blood to blur Phil's tough-guy image.

But soon, there was more than just a little blood. Red was becoming the dominant color on both his chin and his blue shirt. His breathing sounded more and more labored.

But Phil's first concern remained the *Cornelia Marie*.

"My dad always put the boat first before his own health," Josh said.

Finally, Phil conceded this could be far more serious than any of the countless injuries, including many broken bones, he'd suffered over the years.

This was a man who was once in extreme pain from an abscessed tooth while in Dutch Harbor. With no dentist within eight hundred miles, Phil ordered an emergency medical technician to remove the tooth with a pair of pliers, a claw hammer, and a chisel without the benefit of anesthesia.

Grudgingly, he had to admit that this time he was in need of more than a pair of pliers. He agreed to cut short the trip, no small concession for Phil, and head for St. Paul Island, largest of the four Pribilof Islands, located north of the Aleutians. From there, he was flown to Anchorage, 775 miles away.

It didn't take extensive tests for doctors in Anchorage to realize this was a man in serious need of a stress-free environment, a healthy lifestyle, rest, and exercise. They wanted to take away two of Phil's greatest joys, fishing and cigarettes. He was grounded indefinitely and told to quit smoking.

He tentatively agreed to go home to Seattle to recuperate, but give up smoking? No way.

Phil wasn't about to give up his more serious vices either, as Mary was to discover when she came to visit him on his first night back in the fifth wheel at Lake Connor. She stayed over, waking him every hour because he was still coughing up blood and she wanted to make sure it didn't seep into his lungs.

When Mary came in to check on him one time, she caught him doing coke.

"Damn you!" she yelled. "What's wrong with you?"

Phil had alarming health issues, and he paired them with an equally alarming tendency to deny reality.

"He never took care of himself," Mary said.

Nevertheless, being off the boat at least removed the stress of his job. It was absolutely what Phil needed at that point in his life. It just wasn't what his heart and soul demanded. He was Captain Phil Harris, and crab fishing had defined him long before fame had come his way.

Phil may have been the star attraction on *Deadliest Catch*, but nobody connected with the show was rooting for him to return anytime soon.

"He wasn't well and we were really concerned," said Thom Beers, the show's executive producer. "Concerned about him, not the show. We loved it when the doctor told Phil he had to stand down. It was amazing that the guy had even lived through that first attack."

Phil later admitted to his friend Mike Crockett that even he was surprised that he'd survived.

"He smoked more cigarettes in a day," said Phil's father, Grant, "than most people did in a month. And he did it day after day."

Though he knew the futility of trying to change his son, Grant tried.

"How much longer do you think you can do this?" Grant would ask him. Grant already knew the answer, and it scared him.

Phil's friends also appealed to him.

"Phil knew that he needed to cut down on his smoking, but it wasn't going to happen," said custom design artist Mike Lavallee. "I told him, 'You've got to be careful. You need to ease off on all this stuff you're taking. It almost killed you this time. You dodged a bullet.'"

Phil would growl, "I know, I know."

It was his standard response, a way to placate friends, but nothing more.

Because his shop was inundated with paint fumes from floor to ceiling, Lavallee prohibited smoking on the premises, but he made an exception for Phil.

"Whenever he left here," Lavallee said, "it was like the place was on fire."

When Phil was nervous, he would light up three or four cigarettes and keep them all going at the same time, a nicotine juggler.

It wasn't hard to spot the remains of Phil Harris's cigarettes: they had distinctive marks on them because he didn't like dangling a cigarette from his lips. Instead, he kept it firmly gripped in his teeth. If Phil didn't finish his smoke, he would offer it to his friends. But after they saw the trademark punctures down each side, Phil got no takers.

"I remember one of the last nights I was with him," said his friend Jeff Sheets. "We went to the Tulalip Casino. Phil was really nervous that night. His leg was jiggling a hundred miles an hour and he was chomping down on a cigarette. That's how he coped with things."

Nowhere more so than in his wheelhouse. Phil would get in there, kick off his shoes, put on his flip-flops, make sure the windows were tightly shut, turn up the heat, crank up the music, and light up his cigarette.

His lair was nicknamed the "cigarette sauna" by *Deadliest Catch* producer Jeff Conroy. It would be eighty-five degrees in there with no ventilation, the cigarette smoke sometimes so thick the wheelhouse looked like a London street on a foggy morning.

While removing him from the cigarette sauna certainly figured to improve Phil's health, removing the key items in his diet would have been just as beneficial. His favorite foods were jumbo hot dogs, pizzas, and barbecued pork. He loved greasy food, the greasier the better, and washed down most meals with sodas or a cold brew.

"He had the worst diet ever," said Tony Lara, relief skipper/ engineer on the *Cornelia Marie*. "And he never really reflected on the effect it might have on him.

"Maybe that changed when he got sick. But before that, it was high speed all the time, balls to the walls."

Phil's time on hiatus was a period of great frustration, and reminders of his new limitations often caused that frustration to boil over. One such moment came on a trip Phil and Russ took to Las Vegas for an appearance by Phil at a motocross race. As they were driving down the Vegas Strip, Phil got a call informing him that Sig had been selected to be the 2008 grand marshal of the Seattle Seafair.

Along with the designation came the opportunity to ride with the Blue Angels, the Navy and Marine flying acrobats.

Being Seafair grand marshal was a big honor to those living in the Northwest. Others selected have included Seattle Seahawks coach Mike Holmgren and quarterback Warren Moon, speedskater Apolo Ohno, a Seattle native, and comedian Drew Carey.

But what bothered Phil the most was that Sig was getting into a Blue Angels cockpit ahead of him. Phil loved to push the boundaries, whether it was roaring through the Bering Sea or down a Bothell highway. To him, the Blue Angels offered the ultimate thrill ride, a trip to the outer limits.

"Get me on the Blue Angels," he had been telling Russ for a while, "before anybody else."

As Phil hung up his phone in the car, he let out a loud "F-u-u-u-ck."

"The more guttural it was," said Russ, remembering his friend's speech pattern, "and the longer he sustained the vowels, the angrier he was."

Looking over at his fuming companion, Russ asked, "What's wrong?"

"Fucking Sig," said Phil. "He's riding with the Blue Angels. I told you to get me on one of those planes first."

"Phil, I called the commander of the Blue Angels," said Russ. "He is not going to let a guy who had a pulmonary embolism dive at a force of three Gs at five thousand feet in a flight suit only to have another embolism and die. So I'm sorry, but I tried."

Phil was pissed off all day.

Barred from the Bering Sea on doctor's orders, Phil hung out at his trailer, built his beloved birdhouses, worked on the grounds surrounding the fifth wheel, and still smoked like a 1959 Buick with bad piston rings. At least he wasn't completely off the show. *Deadliest Catch* cameras kept America in touch with their favorite captain through frequent airings of his activities and progress.

During this time, he surreptitiously broke all the rules doctors had placed on him, but he acted like the perfect patient when he was around them in order to get the medical release he so desperately wanted in order to return to the boat.

Phil figured he could tough it out. Those who knew him well expected nothing less of him.

"I want to go back," he told Thom.

"No," insisted Thom. "Just stay home."

Phil didn't listen to Thom, didn't listen to his family, didn't listen to his friends. The pull of the sea trumped them all. Phil decided to go back to the Bering Sea in 2009, assuring doctors he would keep all harmful substances out of his body.

Good luck with that, said anybody who knew Phil.

Nevertheless, he was going to return to his favorite place in the world, the wheelhouse of the *Cornelia Marie*.

"Are you coming back too early?" asked Keith Colburn, captain of the *Wizard*.

"Yeah," said Phil, lowering his eyes. "I probably am."

He made it through that year at sea, but it was obvious that the personal storms he had battled in life had battered him far more severely than anything he had encountered at sea.

On December 15, 2009, Phil came to see Mary at her apartment in Bellevue, east of Seattle. When she asked him how he was feeling, Phil bragged that he was down to three cigarettes a day.

"He told me he was sorry he had kept the boys from me for all those years," Mary said, "and that he was going to try to make my life better."

Phil presented her with a gold and ruby ring and offered to pay for her to go back to school.

Then he again asked Mary the question he had first asked thirty-one years earlier: Would she marry him?

It was as if Phil knew that the party was over, and he wanted to go home with the girl he had brought.

Mary turned him down. "You are a much better friend," she said, "than a husband."

Phil understood and walked out the door. It was the last time Mary ever saw him.

CHAPTER 14

THE FINAL VOYAGE

When he left, it was like a hole in the universe was created that nobody will ever be able to fill.

—Lynn Andrews

Whenever the captain was about to head back up north to chase the crab, Lynn, who cleaned his fifth wheel and occasionally cooked for him, would come by to "batten the hatches," as she would describe it. That meant removing the rotten-smelling leftovers inevitably found in the fridge, cleaning up the perennial mess, and locking everything up.

After doing her chores prior to Phil's departure in January 2010 for what would prove to be his last trip up north, Lynn sat around on the porch with Phil, Jake, and several others.

Phil could be a gruff boss, but Lynn had long ago seen through the bluster to the good-hearted soul at his core. But even she was surprised at how openly grateful and complimentary he was that day.

"I just want you to know," Phil told her, "I'm really happy that you work for me. You do a good job and I'm very appreciative."

He then handed Lynn a small white box. Inside was a sapphire stone.

"I wanted you to have something to remember the old captain by," said Phil.

"What do you mean, *remember?*" said Lynn. "You're just going to Alaska."

It was a conversation she'll never forget.

"Phil had never talked like that before," said Lynn after he died. "It just didn't feel right. Maybe he had a premonition something was going to happen."

To this day, Lynn keeps the stone in a safe, but every once in a while, when she misses having Phil in her life, she takes the sapphire out and gazes at it, thinking of him.

Joe Wabey, Phil's first captain, came to visit him on the *Cornelia Marie* just before he pulled up anchor for his last voyage.

There was a look of joy on Phil's face as he watched the *Deadliest Catch* film crew installing their cables and adjusting their cameras. Soon, Phil knew, those cameras would be focused on him, showing him on the high seas where he belonged.

Joe didn't share the happiness of his friend of thirty-six years. Looking into Phil's face, Joe could see a weariness beyond Phil's years, a man in an alarming state of decline. "You don't have to do this," Joe said. "Why don't you just get yourself well, starting with giving up smoking?"

"Are you kidding me?" snapped Phil. "My lungs were tested and they are so good I can absorb all the oxygen I need."

"You are so full of shit," Joe told him. "Five packs a day and you're okay?"

Before he left, Phil called Mike Crockett, admitting that, while he loved the idea of returning to the ocean, he hated opilio fishing.

"Then don't go," Mike told him.

"I got to do this," Phil insisted.

When Phil got back on board the *Cornelia Marie*, it was soon obvious he didn't belong there. His characteristic nervousness, evident even in the best of times, was now amped up to an alarming degree. Josh could see the stress ingrained in his father.

Jake didn't help the situation when he attempted to steal a few pain pills from his father's quarters to feed his addiction, but was caught by Phil. Jake's use of drugs and alcohol had been a constant source of tension with his father for about six years, but when he got caught with his hand in the prescription drug jar he felt the full wrath of Phil's anger. Jake broke down and admitted to his father, in front of a *Deadliest Catch* camera and a worldwide audience, "I'm an addict."

"Dad and I were glad," said Josh, "that Jake was finally being honest with us and, perhaps for the first time, with himself as well."

"Then go to treatment," Phil told Jake. "That's the only thing that's going to save your ass."

For once, Jake listened, agreeing to check into a rehabilitation clinic in Seattle when the trip was over.

While that eased Phil's tension a bit, Josh remained concerned about his father's uncharacteristic sleeping pattern on the trip. As long as Josh could remember, Phil never slept more than two hours a night when he was at sea, awakening with a full supply of energy. Then, when the boat would come into port to unload its crab, he would catch up on the lost hours of sleep. Unlike in his younger days when he would party away the time in the harbor, Phil, by then in his fifties, would be sound asleep for the full sixteen to twenty hours the boat was docked.

But on his first trip back from his year of recuperation, Phil spent much of the time at sea in bed. He'd sleep eight hours, then pull himself up and try to retake command of the ship, but it was obviously difficult. He dragged himself around the boat, struggling just to keep his eyes open.

"I thought it was really weird the way he was acting," Josh said.

One night, as the *Cornelia Marie* headed toward St. Paul to offload its catch, the *Wizard* was leaving the island after bringing in its load of crab.

Captain Keith Colburn vividly remembers the moment when their two ships passed a few hours out of St. Paul. Their radios remained silent, no words spoken, both captains busy in their respective wheelhouses.

"I'm kicking myself to this day that we never even spoke," said Keith.

There was, of course, no way for him to know at the time that it was the last chance he would ever get to speak to Phil.

When the *Cornelia Marie* docked at St. Paul, Phil went to bed, saying he'd be sleeping in the next morning. The rest of the crew got up at dawn, but eight hours later, Phil's door was still shut. When some maintenance issues arose, Steve Ward, the engineer, called him in his stateroom.

No answer.

Ward went up to wake Phil, and within a minute Josh got an urgent call.

"Get up here now," Ward said firmly.

When Josh arrived, he was horrified.

"My dad was lying on the floor in a contorted position," he said. "His left leg was twisted at a perpendicular angle. His left arm was also in an awkwardly bent position."

A hundred-pound bench that had been bolted to the wall was beside Phil. He had apparently ripped it off with his last burst of strength as he fell.

He was muttering as if drunk. The left side of his face seemed frozen and distorted. Josh assumed that was the result of forcefully hitting the floor. But when he and Ward gingerly turned Phil over, they realized the paralysis extended all the way down the left side of Phil's body.

Josh ran downstairs and found Jake in the galley.

"There's been a problem," Josh told his brother. "Don't freak out. Just go upstairs and sit with Dad. I need you to talk to him."

Josh called 911, and paramedics soon arrived at the dock. Just getting Phil off the boat was going to be no easy task. He was heavy to begin with, and his paralysis made it even harder to move him.

Josh knew it would be easier to handle his father if Phil was cooperative, but even in his diminished state, that was only going to happen if he felt comfortable leaving the *Cornelia Marie* in the hands of his crew.

"Once he understood I was going to take care of the boat," Josh said, "he left without a fight."

Phil was strapped to a backboard and then tied into a basket, the type used to hoist stranded sailors up from the ocean or from disabled boats into rescue helicopters.

Everything hanging on the walls had to be removed and all the furniture moved just to get Phil out of his room. The stairs on the *Cornelia Marie*, as on nearly all fishing boats, are steep and set in a passageway so narrow that the shoulders of a man Phil's size would normally brush the walls on either side as he moved.

At one point, it was so tight that he had to be stood straight up, backboard and all, to get him through.

He was taken up to the wheelhouse, where the basket was attached to the crane that Phil had used for so many years to move pots around. Now it was being used to enable the captain of the *Cornelia Marie* to leave his ship for the final time.

He was lowered to the deck, quickly transferred to the ambulance on the dock, and taken to the only hospital on the island.

With a population of around 500, St. Paul had just one doctor and a sparse amount of medical equipment. One crab boat captain referred to the treatment procedures at the hospital as "voodoo medicine."

Fortunately, Phil was medevaced out that same night and flown to the Providence Alaska Medical Center in Anchorage, Alaska's largest hospital. There, doctors determined that he had suffered a massive stroke.

As Phil lay on what would become his deathbed, Thom Beers found himself in an awkward position. On one hand, the star of the hit show he was producing was dying, and millions of viewers around the world wanted to be with a man they had come to know and admire, even if it was only through the lens of a camera.

But, having spent much of the previous seven years working with Phil, and then Josh and Jake, Thom and his fellow producers felt like they were part of the Harris family. Families respect the privacy of each member.

"We weren't just interlopers," said Thom, "who were going to walk in and say, 'Hey, you're dying. Can we film it?'"

He talked with Josh and Jake and told them, "We would like to film everything but won't air anything until all of us, including, hopefully, your dad, make a decision on what is proper and respectful."

With the boys still considering the options and Thom thinking it might be better to back off, Phil, watching the uncertainty from his bed, did what he always did: took command of the operation. Unable to speak coherently, he motioned for paper and pen and scrawled, "You've got to finish the story. It needs an ending."

This is amazing, thought Thom. In the condition he's in, he's producing the show. That took some of the burden of proceeding off Thom, but it still wasn't easy.

Emergency brain surgery was performed to relieve intracranial pressure and swelling.

"Our cameras were there when they opened up his skull," Thom said. "Oh my God, it was so tough."

To ease the awkwardness of being in the room while Phil fought for his life and to avoid intruding too much into the delicate work being performed by doctors, the *Deadliest Catch* film crew tried to focus much of the time on Josh and Jake as they tried to cope with their father's dire situation. They used camera angles that would allow the audience to hear Phil without seeing him.

Russ Herriott, Phil's business manager, was having dinner with friends in Temecula, California, when his cell phone rang. He reached into his pocket and saw the area code was 907.

He knew that was Alaska but didn't recognize the number and

remembered Phil and the boys were out in the Bering Sea, so he stuck the phone back in his pocket without answering it.

"I later felt terrible about that," Russ said. "Big-time regret for a long time."

The guilt first hit him the following morning around nine thirty when he got a text message from George Neighbors, a Discovery Channel executive.

"If there's anything you need, anything we can do, just let me know," wrote Neighbors.

Russ was puzzled. If this was a joke, it was lost on him.

"You want to do something for us?" he wrote back. "How about increasing our pay?"

Russ was always joking with Neighbors about how underpaid he felt Phil was as the star of the show.

Seconds later, Russ's phone rang. It was Neighbors.

"You didn't hear?" he said.

"Didn't hear what?"

"Phil's in the hospital. He had a major stroke."

Standing in a grocery store, Russ froze, speechless. He had become so close to Phil, and yet he felt like he was the last to know. Russ managed to reach Jake at the hospital but still found it difficult to express his feelings.

When Phil's old motorcycle partner Dan Mittman heard that Phil had suffered a stroke, he stuffed a pair of jeans, some underwear, and a couple of shirts into a duffel bag and hopped the first plane to Anchorage.

Russ stayed behind. "I was told by everybody around Phil not to bother going up," Russ said, "because they knew that, if I was there, he was going to start freaking out.

"He was an excitable guy. If he saw me, he would want to have a business meeting right next to the bed. He'd be asking me, 'What do we have going? Am I still doing that bike deal? Are we still doing this? Are we still doing that?'"

But, immediately following the surgery, Phil wasn't asking anything. He lay in an induced coma for three days in the hospital's intensive-care unit.

Medical personnel had warned those around him that Phil might not be able to speak for perhaps weeks after he awoke from the coma. Instead, when his eyes opened, he began talking within a few hours after ripping off his oxygen mask.

"The guy was a fighter," Josh said. "He never stopped."

The moment Dan entered Phil's room on the day the captain came out of his coma, Phil's heart monitor started spiking.

"You must be a very good friend of his," said a nurse as she smiled at the man who considered himself Phil's blood brother.

When Dan shouted, "Phil!" the captain's haggard face broke into a wide smile, a slight sparkle in his once-brilliant eyes. But Dan was not reassured by either the heart monitor or the smile. His first thought was that he'd never seen Phil look so worn out, so fragile.

Still, with the pressure on his brain relieved and the coma ended, Phil was improving enough to start rehab.

"I thought it was amazing," said Jeff Conroy, "that this man was going to get a second chance at life. Or actually, in his case, considering the earlier embolism, a third chance."

Phil was soon talking about making a September comeback, the show about his triumphant return to the Bering Sea already playing in his head.

To doctors, that might have seemed an unrealistic scenario, but to family and friends, it seemed like the next logical chapter in an already legendary life. After all, this was a man who had risen faster, lived more dangerously, and succeeded more spectacularly than almost any other crab captain. He had always scoffed at the limits set by others.

On camera, Phil remained the tough, courageous sea captain as though his deteriorating condition was just another big wave he had to get over. At times, he seemed like an actor, the leading man on a blockbuster show merely reading lines in a script that would ultimately lead to his demise.

Enmeshed in tubes, with needles penetrating his body and machines beeping his status, Phil kept snarling, "Get me a cigarette," to anyone who might listen.

"He was still incorrigible, right to the very end," said Thom, marveling at the man's fortitude.

It should not have been surprising that he continued to project his tough-guy persona. After all, he had faced the specter of death many times throughout his life, whether on the high seas or the back roads of Bothell, and always survived. And each time, the aura of invincibility around him seemed to grow.

But in the quiet of his hospital room, when the ever-present cameras were turned off, Phil conveyed to Dan severe misgivings this time about his future.

He conceded that he wasn't sure how much of the Phil Harris the world had come to know and admire was left in his body. He looked into Dan's eyes and lamented that he'd never ride a motorcycle again. He shared his belief that he was destined to end his days outfitted in diapers. Dan's heart sank as he listened to Phil admit that his spirit was withering at the possibility of being forced to live out his remaining days as little more than a vegetable.

It was painful for Dan to watch a man who had laughed in the face of death on a daily basis now fight off tears at the prospect of living as an invalid.

In those final conversations with Dan, Phil's emotions soared and plunged. He would try to recapture his old resolve, vowing to face his condition with the same confidence and optimism he had exuded in facing a killer wave dead ahead. But that resolve kept faltering as the gravity of his medical condition sank in. He would succumb to spells of depression as he grudgingly came to terms with the idea that his body had betrayed him. But then, he would rally again. He would tell

Dan he was going to find a way to survive this devastating stroke, that Captain Phil Harris was going to find a safe harbor because, damn it, Jake and Josh needed him.

The staff at the hospital treated Dan well, recognizing that his steadfast presence could play a key role in bringing about their patient's recovery. So while the staff chased away most visitors at the conclusion of visiting hours, they made an exception for Dan. It was probably a moot point because, where Phil was concerned, Dan stood firm. It would take a backhoe to remove him.

By February 7, Super Bowl Sunday, Phil was able to focus his mind sufficiently to watch the New Orleans Saints beat the Indianapolis Colts, getting engrossed in the game as he had in so many others on those long, happy football afternoons in the fifth wheel at Lake Connor.

The next day, Russ was told that Phil had progressed so much that arrangements were under way to airlift him down to Seattle.

Phil was told he was going to have to wear a helmet during the flight to protect the area of his skull where the surgery had been performed. Ever the participant, never just the observer, Phil, even in his life-threatening state, had to be involved in the process. Not just any helmet would do, he told doctors. He wanted a blue helmet, *Cornelia Marie* blue.

"But we don't have that color," he was told.

"Then paint one," Phil demanded.

Who comes out of a coma making demands?

"Painting the helmet will take a couple of days," a hospital official told Phil.

"I can wait," he said.

Josh was dealing with a much bigger problem than a painted helmet. To airlift Phil down to Seattle was going to cost around twenty thousand dollars, an expense he and his family were going to have to bear.

Calling around in search of a cheaper flight, Josh found a company willing to cut the famous captain a deal.

"The fuel will cost around forty-five hundred dollars," Josh was told. "Pay for that and we'll fly him down there for free."

That made a perennial bargain hunter like Phil proud of his son.

On February 9, the winter winds of Anchorage swept across the grey city, as relentless and biting as a pit bull. The swirling cold didn't discourage Dan. He merely tightened the collar of his army jacket and pushed on along the icy sidewalks in what had become a familiar, though still unpleasant, march. Dan was heading for Providence Alaska Medical Center, just as he had each of the previous ten days.

When he reached room 205, Phil's room, Dan was surprised to find it filled with people. Along with the usual doctors and nurses running tests and reading monitors, there were several physical therapists getting Phil ready to stretch his muscles and then leave his bed for a big outing to test his legs and stamina, a walk to the nurses' station and back.

Dan waved to Phil, told him he'd be back after the workout, and then meandered around the large building.

Phil had charmed the hospital staff into looking the other way when he wanted to break the rules, but they wouldn't budge when it came to nicotine. So, when Jake arrived at the hospital earlier that morning to say good-bye, Phil, figuring he had a soft touch, greeted his son by asking for a cigarette. Jake, showing his new inner strength and resolve, turned his father down.

"You're sneaky, but I can't do it," Jake said.

"I just want one," pleaded Phil.

"I know, one after another," said Jake. "I'm going to be a nonsmoker myself in a little bit. I just got hold of the rehab center today and made the arrangements to go in for help. I'm still going to keep my promise."

"Hey, I'm real proud of you," said Phil, kissing his son's knuckles.

"Thank you," replied Jake, soaking in the words he had longed to hear.

"Thank *you*," said Phil.

"I don't want to leave you," Jake said, "but this is for the better."

"Yeah, it is," Phil agreed.

"You just keep on doin' what you're doin'," Jake told him.

Phil again assured his son that his actions had brought some welcome joy into Phil's long, bleak days.

"That's what I like to hear," Jake said. "I'll give you a call when I hit Seattle. I love you, Pops."

As he left the room, Jake turned for one last, lingering look at his dad. It is the parting image he will carry with him for the rest of his life.

With Jake gone, the responsibility for standing vigil over Phil was solely on Josh's shoulders. He welcomed it as an opportunity to solidify a bond with his father that had so often been tenuous in the past.

Bolstering that desire was the news he brought when he came to his father's bedside. All the arrangements were complete. The flight home to Seattle was a go.

"We're taking you home, Dad," he said. "The pilots are doing it for free because they like us, so be nice to them."

"Get me my crab necklace," Phil ordered his son, referring to his favorite piece of jewelry.

"But, Dad," Josh said, "they won't let you wear any jewelry when you're all hooked up like that."

"Just go get it," said Phil.

The jewelry was in Josh's hotel room. Before he left to retrieve it, he reached out for his father's hand, remembering how his dad had taken his hand when he was a child and his little world was in crisis.

In healthier times, the macho Phil might have slapped away an adult son's hand, deeming it unmanly to show affection in such a manner. But now, desperate to maintain a link with his flesh and blood, Phil welcomed the hand, squeezing it with all his remaining strength.

"Okay, we know you've got power," said Josh with a smile.

"I'm sorry," Phil told his son.

"Why?" asked Josh.

"When you were growing up, I should have been a better father," Phil said.

"No way," said Josh. "You've been the best father you ever could have been. You taught me great skills, everything I need to know to be a man. So don't ever say that. Don't ever apologize, Dad. And now, I'm gonna take care of you as best as I possibly can. I'm not going to let you out of my sight. Same thing you'd do for me."

Tears formed in Phil's eyes, quickly brushed away by his son.

"I love you, buddy," Josh said.

"I love you, too," responded Phil.

"I know. I'm being strong here," said Josh.

Phil put his hands on his lips and then tried to touch Josh's lips. Josh responded by kissing his father's forehead.

Josh hated to cry, especially in front of his father. He flicked a tear of his own away and fled the room, motioning the *Deadliest Catch* cameraman not to follow him. This reality show had gotten too real for him.

As Phil was being carefully taken out of bed for his brief walk, Dan was in another wing of the hospital where he had struck up a conversation with the security chief. It was then that an uneasy feeling came over Dan, a feeling he couldn't shake: Phil needed him.

He quickly made his way back to room 205, where he found Phil totally exhausted after his brief walk and his conversations with his two sons. He was irritated and somewhat confused.

"I'm hot," he told Dan.

"Well yeah, you got your fat ass out of bed for the first time since

you got here," said Dan, trying to ease his friend back into the typical
banter between the two that had always brought a smile to Phil's face.
"You took three steps to the toilet, so hell yeah, you're gonna get tired."

Beyond consoling, Phil yelled, "They wore me out!"

A male nurse named Dave came in and reattached Phil's arm to
an IV tube. As Dave worked, Dan kept talking, hoping to take Phil's
mind off his increasing distress. Dan reminded his old friend that they
would be heading home the next day, bound for Seattle's Swedish
Medical Center, located between I-5 and Lake Washington, southwest
of Bothell. Dan brought up all those familiar places along with many
of the haunts where the two had had so many good times, reinforcing
the idea that Phil was going back to the familiarity of the area where
he had lived his entire life.

"Just chill," said Dan. "If you settle down and make it back home,
everything will be fine."

But everything wasn't fine. He could tell from the desperation he
saw on Phil's face and the tone of his voice that something was seriously wrong.

Phil barked out, "I'M HOT! I'M HOT! I'M HOT!"

Then he started to convulse. With tears in his eyes, Dan grabbed
him and hollered, "Phil! Phil!"

No response.

Phil's eyes rolled back in his head.

An urgent call sounded through the halls: "Code Blue at wing
E2 . . . 026 . . . room 205." Captain Phil Harris was slipping away.

Medical personnel streamed into the room.

Meanwhile, Josh got back to the hotel, grabbed the necklace, and
dropped it into the left breast pocket of his coat. At the instant he felt
it softly hit the bottom of the pocket, Josh heard his cell phone ring in
his right pocket. It was a hospital administrator telling him, "Your dad
just hit code."

"What does that mean?" asked Josh.

"It means you need to get back here," he was told.

As Josh raced down the frozen Anchorage streets, his cell rang again.

"You really need to step on it," said the voice on the other end.

Dan had talked to Grant that morning, letting him know his son was showing tremendous improvement and would be heading home the next day. And now, Phil was on the verge of death.

When Josh burst into the operating room, he counted sixteen people working on his father. Phil's chest was split wide open and doctors were aggressively performing heart massage.

Josh was advised to wait outside but was updated constantly on his father's condition.

Fifteen minutes went by. Thirty minutes.

Finally, over an hour after the Code Blue had sounded, Dr. Robert Lada, head of Phil's medical team, emerged from the operating room.

"Your dad's dead," he told Josh, softly yet firmly. "If we continue on, we might get vital signs back, but he's going to be brain-dead."

With Jake already on his way to rehab, it was Josh's call.

"That haunts me," said Josh. "It was my decision alone. I was by myself. That sucked. Every day, I wonder if I did the right thing."

He gave the okay to pull the plug. Eleven days after arriving at the Providence Alaska Medical Center, Phil was pronounced dead from an intracranial hemorrhage.

Josh called Jake to give his little brother the horrible news. Phil Harris belonged to the ages, and Jake and Josh Harris were all alone.

When Phil died, Dan grabbed Phil's cell phone, walked to the hospital's rooftop, and hurled the phone over the edge, watching it sail down to the pavement and explode into a million pieces. Then he looked up at the heavens and smiled.

"The toughest part," said Thom, "was that he rallied and we thought he was going to live. And then, we lost him."

At five forty-five on the afternoon of February 10, 2010, Russ was walking into a gym when Mike Lavallee called.

"Is it true?" Mike asked.

"Is what true?"

"That Phil died."

"Phil didn't die," Russ insisted. "They are airlifting him down this week, and I'm going to fly up and see him."

"I just got a call from a guy who knows Jake, who said Phil passed away," insisted Mike.

Russ hung up without even a good-bye and hit the speed dial for Josh. "Dude, it's Russ. What happened?" he asked.

"I can't talk," Josh replied. "I've got to call you right back."

That wasn't necessary. Russ realized his friend was indeed gone.

"It was a miserable rainy day in February and everything had changed," he said.

At her Bellevue apartment, Mary's phone rang. It was Grant.

She had spoken to him the day before when she learned Phil was being flown back to Seattle, offering to take care of her ex-husband.

"How's it going?" Mary asked.

"It's not going so good," Grant replied. Before he uttered another word, Mary knew in her heart the reason for the call.

"Phil's gone," Grant said. "He didn't make it."

"How can that be?" said Mary, slipping into denial. "He was coming home tomorrow."

"Nope, he's not," said Grant.

"But," said Mary, "we had so much more to talk about."

With Phil's death, the final chapter of his life came to a close, but the biggest chapter of *Deadliest Catch* still had to be edited. If it had been a movie, everybody on the set would have known whether they were filming the leading man undergoing a miraculous medical comeback or sinking into the throes of death. All they would have had to do was follow the script.

But this was real life, the ultimate reality show with a shocking, unpredictable climax. As they shot, no one could be sure of what was going to happen. Then the postproduction crew at the studio took on the difficult task of assembling the footage to show the death of their leading man.

"We spent countless hours," said Jeff, "debating what was right and what was wrong and where the line was that we couldn't cross."

One taboo was obvious.

"After part of Phil's skull had been removed, it deflated," Jeff said, "so he had a very concave-looking head. We were determined not to put that on the air. We were not going to show him in a gruesome way."

"There were times when we were editing the show, reviewing so many powerful moments, that we had to stop," Jeff said, "because we were emotionally drained."

The production crew would put everything on pause, leave the room, take a deep breath, and compose themselves after scenes like the one in which Phil apologizes to Josh for not always being a good father.

The first season of *Deadliest Catch* averaged between 2 and 3 million viewers an episode, and that's the way it stayed for six seasons until Phil's death. Every fan of the show, from the most devoted to the most casual, and even countless numbers who had never watched *Deadliest Catch* yet had heard of Captain Phil Harris, knew that he had died. When the episode in which he passed away aired on July 13, 2010, five months after Phil's death, 8.5 million viewers tuned in.

"Public opinion about the show was very positive," Jeff said. "We had expected to be heavily criticized, that we would get a lot of backlash because we had filmed a person passing away. I can't deny there was a degree of exploitation, but we tried to nullify that by presenting an honest look at this man and his life as much as his death."

It is a show Thom is extremely proud of. "We wanted to cover the death of an international figure with as much class as we possibly could," he said. "We didn't actually show him die. There's no way I would do that. Too much respect. What we showed was a phone call to the boys."

"Frankly," said Joe Wabey, "I'm surprised he lived as long as he did, because he lived so hard and so fast. Alcohol and coke was a bad combo for him, but he had been in denial about his health forever. He'd always say, 'I'm fine. I'm fine.' I never argued with him when he said that. It was his business. He was a big boy. Nobody can tell you how to live. But I'm still sad about his passing three years later, because he was a unique individual in my life."

"Phil was at the top of his game," said Tony Lara, "until that stroke messed him up. I don't want to say his death was for the best, but, had he lived in that condition, he would not have been happy."

Each person whose life Phil touched hangs on to their special connection to him. It's often the little things that linger in their memories.

Grant smiles every time he turns on the late news on Channel 5 in Seattle. When it's the time for the weather report, the newscast switches to a camera on the roof of the station's building that zooms in on a garden overlooking the city. And clearly seen above that garden is a birdhouse, a Phil Harris birdhouse.

"When I think of Phil now," said Russ, "I see him standing in front of the trailer, cigarette in hand, wearing a Harley cut-off shirt and jeans, boots on, hair slicked back like he's ready to go out. And he's saying to me, 'Hey, tough guy, what are you doing today?' Big smile on his face, not a care in the world."

When it came to Josh and Jake, Phil cared a lot. Now that he is gone, every time an opportunity arises for them they can only guess what advice he would give them.

"Phil would like to see them succeed, of course," said Joe, "but he would want them to be happy by being involved in something they enjoy. He wouldn't have been insistent that they remain crab fishermen and run a boat unless it was what they wanted to do. He knew how tough a job it can be."

"Phil's two boys were his life," said Mike Crockett. "I believe it would have given him the ultimate satisfaction to live long enough to see each of his sons get past their vicious cycle of party, trouble, party, trouble, and to settle down, establish a career, have a family, and give him grandkids.

"There was more to come in his life. He loved being a celebrity and living the high life, but beyond that, he wanted to be with his family."

Nobody, of course, took the loss harder than Jake and Josh. After his father's death, Jake, emulating Phil's own daring dashes with the law in pursuit, got involved in a high-speed chase through downtown Seattle involving a posse of squad cars.

When they cornered him, Jake remained defiant.

"They had their guns drawn," he said, "and one of them just ripped me out of the window and threw me on the ground.

"I had basically lost it over my dad's death. When the police let me up, they told me they were sorry about my father. They probably should have kicked my ass, but they were cool."

The judge wasn't so forgiving. Jake had to spend a week in jail.

"At first, you just want to drown the sorrow in booze," remembers Jake. "But then, you learn to balance the sadness with the realization that you were fortunate to have had the time with him that you did. You focus on remembering the good things. It's a process that you have to take in baby steps. But the feeling of loss will never leave me."

One snapshot of his years with his father remains foremost in Jake's mind.

"There's a really curvy back road near Bothell called High Bridge Road," he said. "I can see myself riding there on the back of Dad's bike, hanging on to him."

His son, his bike, the thrill: it's the perfect Phil Harris moment.

EPILOGUE

BACK IN THE BERING FOREVER

If I could ask one last thing of my dad, it would be, "Tell me a story."

—*Jake*

The fog rolls in, draping the Bothell cemetery in mist. Spread out across the manicured lawns are granite and marble slabs etched with epitaphs.

We are here with Russ Herriott. A few steps off the paved access path, we search for our father's resting spot. It's nearby, but we have trouble finding it because there is no eye-catching headstone.

Half of Dad's ashes were buried here in the same plot where our grandmother lies, a few feet above her. His ashes were encased in twin urns that are actually teardrop-shaped Harley motorcycle gas tanks. Mike Lavallee provided a custom paint job: airbrushed images from our father's life, all in red, his favorite color. One urn, the one we're visiting today, depicts his life on land, from his family to his cycles.

The other one shows the captain at sea. It was deposited in the water in a memorable ceremony and today lies at the bottom of the Bering Sea, right where Dad wanted it. He figured that the tide would carry him wherever he wanted to go.

At Dad's funeral, we felt like figures cast in stone. We participated in the service, but we weren't really there. The reality of losing our dad hadn't fully set in yet, so we didn't appreciate the opportunity to say good-bye.

It is only now, months later, that we're finally ready to pay our respects. That is why we have come to the cemetery.

At last, we find Dad's grave marker. It is simple, the area quiet, a stark contrast to the sound and fury that always seemed to fuel Dad. A few wayward leaves adhere stubbornly to the stone. When Jake drops to his knees to remove them, his fingers linger on the engraved words.

The two of us along with Russ form a circle around the headstone, but there is also someone else here. We all feel it, the fourth presence—Dad.

We take turns stealing deep, ragged breaths. We try to shield our vulnerability, but we know—we see it in one another—that there's no hiding the loss. Our dad is dead, our best friend, our hero, and a truly legendary fisherman.

Yes, he is gone. But millions remember.

We thank every one of you.

Sincerely,
Josh and Jake

ABOUT THE AUTHORS

JOSH AND JAKE HARRIS are Captain Phil's two surviving sons. Both followed their father into crab fishing and are now *Deadliest Catch* stars in their own right. In late 2012, they accomplished a dream three years in the making by purchasing Phil's famous crab boat, the *Cornelia Marie*, which they now co-captain on the Bering Sea and on television screens around the world.

STEVE SPRINGER is a veteran journalist, an award-winning sportswriter, and the author of ten other books, including three bestsellers. He spent twenty-five years as a sportswriter for the *Los Angeles Times* and currently lives in Woodland Hills, California, with his wife and near his kids, their spouses, and two grandsons.

BLAKE CHAVEZ attended California Pacific School of Law and achieved success as a business executive before becoming a professional writer. His previous book with Steve Springer is *Hard Luck*. He lives in California with his wife and daughter.